# OUT OF
# THE
# DELTA

Zeek Taylor

All rights reserved. This book or any portion thereof may not be reproduced or used in any manner whatsoever without the express written permission of the publisher except for the use of brief quotations in a review.

ISBN-13: 978-1537353531

Copyright © 2016 Zeek Taylor

Keezart Press

Eureka Springs, Arkansas

# DEDICATION

This book is dedicated to the many friends and relatives who have been a part of my journey in this life. I also dedicate this book to my parents, Allene and Z. W. Taylor, who always encouraged me to seek my passions and who loved me unconditionally, and to my life partner, Dick Titus, who has stood by me, loved me, and told me, "You can do it."

# CONTENTS

|   | Introduction | 1 |
|---|---|---|
| 1 | Childhood | 3 |
| 2 | Happy Times In Happy Town | 29 |
| 3 | Teen Time | 45 |
| 4. | Family | 65 |
| 5 | From Student to Teacher | 91 |
| 6 | Memphis | 101 |
| 7 | Fayetteville | 121 |
| 8 | Eureka Springs | 135 |

# INTRODUCTION

The stories in this book were originally written as "Throw Back Thursday" posts on Facebook. They are auto-biological tales that begin in the Northeast Arkansas Delta town of Marmaduke. They continue with my journeys through other locations, professions, encounters, and with people that have shaped my life. The stories are in chronological order. Some of the information may overlap and may be repeated. My intent and hope is that each tale will stand alone as a short story, make you laugh or cry, and perhaps inspire you. At the least, I hope they entertain you.

# 1 CHILDHOOD

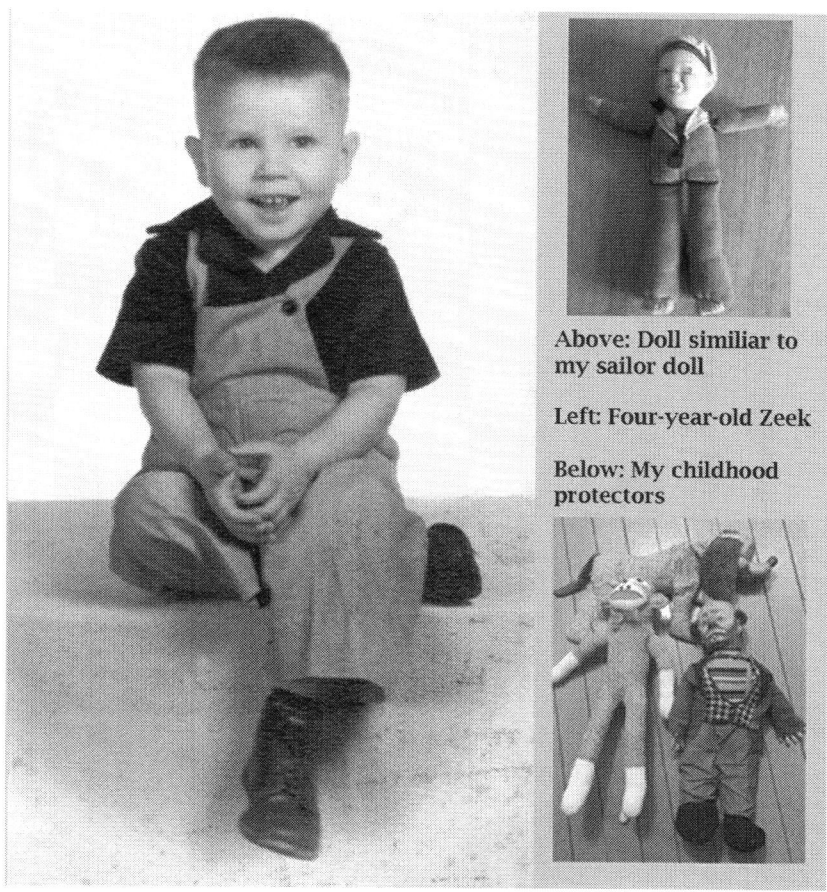

Above: Doll similiar to my sailor doll

Left: Four-year-old Zeek

Below: My childhood protectors

**Protectors:** Until I was four years-old, my parents, two sisters and I slept in a large narrow room. I would scoot my green metal youth bed up against my parents' bed and nestle down between our mattresses. I felt protected. When my sisters and I got a little older, my parents decided it was time that we have separate bedrooms. A wall was built that divided the big room into two rooms. My parents moved into what had been a guest bedroom, and my sisters were given the front part of the newly walled room. I was given the back section. I had my very own room. I was alone at night for the first time, it was dark, and I was scared.

I had seen the movie Pinocchio, and I was terrified by the villains in the film, Honest John and Gideon the Cat. I thought they were hiding underneath my bed at night. I didn't dare look. For my fourth birthday,

I was given a sailor doll. He was dressed in navy blue, and he had a composite head. He was my friend, and I took him everywhere with me. My sailor doll was my protector during dark lonely nights. I was no longer afraid of the dark and the creatures who I thought were under my bed. One day I dropped my sailor doll and his head shattered. I was distraught. After he was broken, I was once again terrified at night until my grandmother made me a sock monkey as a "protector." My fears abated.

I would cover my head at night and snuggle with my sock monkey friend. I felt safe and secure. Soon the sock monkey was joined by a new stuffed animal, a hound dog, and then by a real dog, Jiggs.

One Christmas while looking through the Sears Christmas catalogue, I spotted a Sad Willie clown doll. I asked Santa to bring me Willie. He did. After that Christmas, during the night, I would snuggle underneath the covers with the hound, the clown, and the sock monkey. Jiggs would lie on top of the bedspread up against my legs. I had protection.

At times our guardian angels are "what we make them."

**Christmas Memories:** When I was a very young boy, I claimed Reverend Fern Cook as my girlfriend. Miss Fern was the minister of the Methodist church that we attended. The church and the parsonage were across the alley from my family home. That location allowed me to have frequent visits with the good reverend. If I saw Miss Fern in her yard, I would run across the alley to get a hug.

During the Christmas of my 4$^{th}$ year, I was excited to take Miss Fern a present, an assortment of candies and cookies that my mother had made. I walked across the alley carefully balancing the platter of sweets. My little dog Jiggs was close behind. I knocked and knocked on Miss Fern's door. No answer. The door was unlocked. I decided I would go in and leave the gift as a surprise for my girlfriend.

Jiggs and I entered the parsonage and placed the platter on the dining table. It was then that I saw Miss Fern's beautiful Christmas tree. It was lit with bubble lights and decorated with lovely ornaments and sparkly icicles. I spotted real candy canes on the tree. I took one off the tree and ate it. I took another one from the tree and gave it to Jiggs. I ate another one. Jiggs ate another one. I decided I might as well take the rest of the candy canes home with me. The tree was quite tall, but I was able to reach quite a few to take back across the alley. I went straight to my room and laid the candy on my dresser. My mother came to my room and spotted the candy canes. She wanted to know if Miss Fern had given them to me. I told my mother the truth. My mother sternly informed me that I would return the candy, and I would apologize for my misdeed.

My mother kept going back and forth across the alley to see if the Reverend's car was back in the parsonage's carport. I sat on the couch and waited. Finally, Miss Fern returned home. My mother escorted me across the alley with candy canes in hand. Jiggs stayed home this time. I was concerned that Miss Fern would be mad at me and no longer want to be my girlfriend. That would have meant no more hugs. I was so relieved when the kind Reverend said, "I knew you were coming and Santa and I placed the candy canes on the tree just for you." She then took the rest of the candy off the tree and gave the canes to me. On that day Miss Fern taught me about love, forgiveness, and the true meaning of Christmas.

Above: Marmaduke Methodist Church

**Santa Claus Is Coming to Town:** The Sears Christmas Wish Book came out in early fall during the 1950s. My younger sister and I would spend hours looking at the pictures in the colorful catalogue. We would read each item's description, and carefully make the important decision about what we wanted Santa to bring to us for Christmas. We would write our names on the selected items, and then give the catalogue to my mother. One year I made a decision in short-order. There was a farm set in the wish book complete with a tin barn, fencing, and plastic animals. I had to have it. There was one problem. I was beginning to doubt the existence of Santa. I was afraid if I didn't "believe" then I would not receive the farm set.

It was confusing for me when we would go Christmas shopping, and I would see Santa in more than one store, and all on the same day. I was beginning to doubt my mother's explanation, "They are Santa's helpers." I thought, "Well, then why are they all dressed like Santa?"

I didn't dare mention my doubts to my younger sister. She was unwavering in her belief in the Jolly Ol' Elf. I was afraid to discuss my doubts with my mother for fear that by just questioning out loud Santa's existence, it would prevent me from receiving my dream gift, the farm set.

Every year in December my family attended the nighttime Christmas parade in Paragould, Arkansas. The year of my doubt, as was customary, we bundled up, and drove to the nearby town for the parade. We parked and walked up the street to where the parade would pass, and we secured a good viewing spot. It was then that my mother realized she had lost her purse. Not only had she lost her wallet and the money that was in the purse, she had lost her favorite handbag. It was a hand-tooled tan and red leather bag that my Aunt Betty had brought to her from Casablanca, Morocco. My mother muttered a cuss word, and then said "That's that. It's gone. Just enjoy the parade."

Standing on the curb with my father, two sisters, and my grandmother while waiting for the parade to begin, I felt sorry for my mother. After the parade was under way, I soon was lost in the grandeur of the floats and the precision of the marching bands. I was mesmerized by the twirlers who were bedecked in skimpy holiday outfits and wearing white majorette boots with tassels. I forgot about the lost purse.

The last float was occupied by Santa sitting on a sleigh that was pulled by large illuminated plastic reindeer. When it neared, my mother gasped when she spotted her purse sitting on the front of the float. A Good Samaritan had found it, placed the purse on the front of the float knowing that whoever had lost it would certainly see it. We followed the float to the end of the parade. My mother kept proclaiming, "Santa found my purse." She retrieved her prized handbag while happily thanking Santa Claus. He patted me on the head. My doubt about Santa's existence then went away. He had to be real and have magic to pull off such a feat.

On Christmas morning I found the farm set that Santa had left for me. Believe.

**Smart Dog and Art**: At age five, I wanted to go to school. We did not have kindergarten where I lived. My father was good friends with the superintendent of schools, and as a favor to my daddy, he let me start first grade a year early. My father drove me to school every morning. During the first week after he dropped me off, I would run down alleyways and beat him home. My parents couldn't figure out why I was doing that because I had begged to go to school. I confessed that I didn't want to be away from my dog. I had a sympathetic first grade teacher, Miss Versa Butler, and she let me take my dog Jiggs to school. He sat in a little seat beside me. From then on, I loved school. I told everyone that Jiggs had learned his ABCs, but couldn't say the alphabet out loud because he hadn't yet learned to talk.

I decided to become an artist during the first year in school. I won the grand prize in the first grade art contest with a crayon portrait that I did of my mother. I drew her hair in fabulous circles with a crayon called mahogany, and in the picture I gave her almost perfectly round cheeks with a carnation pink crayon. As the winner, I had my choice of either a big ol' peppermint stick or a Chick-O-Stick, a peanut butter, toasted coconut coated concoction of a stick. I chose the Chick-O-Stick and devoured my prize during the next recess. After winning the contest, there was never any doubt in my mind that I wanted to become an artist. I stuck with my plan.

**Dressing Like a Man:** A couple of weeks after starting the first grade, I noticed with interest and envy that a boy in my class was not wearing suspenders or overalls. Max was wearing a belt. I didn't know that they made belts for little boys. Then, I saw other little boys wearing belts that were just like the ones that grown men wore. By gosh, I wanted one too. I begged and begged my parents for a belt. They finally consented. However, I had to wait until the next weekend to purchase one when we could go to Graber's, a department store in nearby Paragould, Arkansas.

My mother was a hairdresser. Each week when she got through work on Saturday, my family would load into my father's car, and we would go to Paragould to grocery shop at Kroger's. If my mother got through working early enough, we would get there in time to shop in one of the town's department stores before ending up at the grocery store. On the Saturday when I was to get my belt, I was worried she wouldn't get through in time to go to Graber's. I kept running into the beauty shop to see if she was almost done working. I was hoping that her last customer wouldn't take too long under the hairdryer. My mother did get through in time that Saturday for us to make it to the department store to buy the belt. I'm not sure I could have waited another week. The first night I had the belt, I fastened it around my pajama bottoms, and I slept in it. I felt grown-up.

Above: My first grade class. I'm the boy, front row, right side on the end. I have on suspenders prior to getting my belt. Max is standing by our teacher, Miss Versa, and he is wearing a belt.

**Cookies and Kool-Aid:** I grew up in a little Delta town with a population of 650 people. Within the city limits there were five churches. If attended equally that would have averaged 130 residents per church. Although most folks did attend, not everyone was a church goer, at least not on a regular basis. I don't think I ever went to any one church back then that had 130 people in attendance. The town had one Church of Christ, and one Methodist Church. Baptists were in the majority with three churches. Their flocks were split between three branches: General Baptist, Missionary Baptist, and Southern Baptist. Outside the city limits there were many country churches including a few more Baptist congregations.

We were Methodists. My grandfather Taylor was a Methodist minister. However, the only time my father attended our church was when my grandfather was in town. I suspect that my father had his fill of church going while he was growing up. My mother did attend on a regular basis, but she always sat on the back pew and made a beeline for home the minute the preacher said the last "amen." She was anxious to get Sunday dinner on the table. The church was across the alley from our house and she could be home in sixty seconds. My mother's idea of a good preacher was one that gave a short sermon.

My two sisters and I did attend regularly. When small, we mainly went to Sunday school. I liked Sunday school alright because there was a good chance that some kid in the class would have a birthday celebration. When that happened the teacher would run down to Crouch's grocery store and buy vanilla wafers and little tubs of vanilla ice-cream that we ate with wooden spoons.

Another perk of Sunday school is that we got to color mimeographed pictures of Biblical scenes. I didn't care what the subject matter was as long as I could take advantage of the dozens of crayons available to me. There were colors in the Sunday school classroom that I didn't have at home.

When I got a little older, I opted to stay home and watch African-American church services that were broadcast on television via Memphis stations. I only watched for the music, and I turned off the TV when the preaching came on. My mother didn't mind if I stayed home. It was my choice. However, I was not to go out of the house on Sunday morning in case some good church goer might see me, and wonder why I wasn't in church.

During summer my church hosted a week-long vacation Bible school. I loved going mainly for the cookies, Kool-Aid, and the crafts. One of the Baptist churches was directly across the alley from our house, and they also hosted a vacation Bible school. One year the Baptist preacher came a-calling and invited my sisters and me to attend. My older sister told him that we couldn't because, "We are Methodists." That didn't stop me. I knew that the Baptists also had cookies, Kool-Aid, and crafts.

I started going to both vacation Bible schools when I was five-years-old. When I was in the first grade class at the Baptist Bible school, each student was given a line of scripture to learn. The line was to be recited at a program performed at the end of the Bible school. Each year the program was held at night in the church sanctuary, and it was heavily attended by beaming parents, grandparents, and family friends.

The line that I was given was, "The Lord is my Shepherd." I was only to recite the one line. I misunderstood and thought that I was to memorize the entire 23rd Psalm. I practiced and practiced until I had it down pat. The night of the program, my entire family was in attendance. Each of my classmates recited their one line. I recited the entire 23rd Psalm and I received a large round of applause.

When we got home, my oldest sister wagged her finger at me and said, "You were just trying to show off in front of the Baptists. You are nothing but a show off." My mother stepped in and said, "No, he is just an overachiever." I asked her if that was a good thing? She said, "Yes."

Thereafter the term "overachiever" stuck in my mind. At least she didn't call me "adorably precocious," or a "ham." Bless my mother's heart.

When I was six-years-old my teacher during that summer's Baptist Bible School was Miss Betty. There were ten students in my class. Miss Betty had a baby boy who was a few-months-old, and she brought him to class with her. One morning the baby was fussy, and to stop his crying, Miss Betty opened her blouse and pulled out a very large breast and proceeded to nurse the baby. I was fascinated. I had never seen an uncovered breast.

When I returned home from Bible School that day, my mother was somewhat shocked when I answered her question, "What did you learn today?" I replied, "Miss Betty's boobie is bigger than my head."

It took a lot of begging on my part before my mother consented to let me return to the school the next day. I felt lucky to be there. Half of the kids were absent due to the "exposure." It was difficult for me to pay attention that morning. I kept looking at the sleeping baby boy and hoping that he would wake up and cry. However, no such luck.

Above: Young Zeek
Right: Ice cream
Above: Baptist Church and Methodist Church, Marmaduke, AR

**The Hottest of Dogs:** In the small Delta town of Marmaduke, Arkansas, there was a grocery store, Crouch's, and it was a few doors down and across the street from our home. Every afternoon after school my sister and I were each given a dime to go to the store and buy a coke and a candy bar. We would take empty coke bottles with us to trade for the new full bottles. Without a trade-in bottle, we had to pay an extra two cents deposit on top of the nickel cost of the coke.

I thought it was fun to have my younger sister tell me what kind of candy bar that she wanted. She could not say Butterfinger. I asked her every day, and her answer was always the same, "A Butterthinger." That amused me to no end.

The store had groceries, was a gathering place for locals, and it was located directly across the street from the town's city hall and jail. The jail had been featured in the Arkansas Gazette newspaper as the only jail in the state with a cell that had a picture window adorned with homemade curtains. Crouch's grocery, owned by Viola and Bus Crouch, was the perfect place to watch comings and goings at city hall and the jail.

Viola was one of my mother's best friends, and she always treated the Taylors as family. She and Bus lived in a nice large house that was catty-corner from the store. Every week Viola walked the block to my mother's beauty shop to get her weekly shampoo and set. She had a standing appointment for several decades.

Above: Viola in Crouch's Grocery Store.

Connected to the grocery store on one end was a service station. Connected to the store on the other end was a café complete with a jukebox and a pinball machine. The café had an entrance from the store. The food was home cooked. The menu included open faced beef or pork sandwiches complete with mashed potatoes, gravy, and slaw. The meal cost fifty cents. I spent a lot of time and many nickels playing the juke box and pinball machine in the restaurant. For several decades, my family went to Crouch's, to buy groceries, eat in the café, get gas for the car, or just to visit.

When I was four-years-old, my Aunt Betty, Uncle Leroy, and cousins came to visit my family. While they were there, my six-year-old sister Cheryl, my five-year-old cousin LeJean, and I decided to have a wiener roast.

We took some hot dogs from my mother's refrigerator, and we took them to the backyard. We decided the best place to make a fire for the wiener roast was in a doghouse that my daddy had built for his bird dog, Old Tip. The doghouse was built inside a shed that was connected to the garage that housed the family car. Tip's house was filled with easily ignited, highly combustible straw.

My cousin and I had a penny. We went across the street to Crouch's, and purchased a one cent box of matches. Viola was suspicious of the reason for our purchase. She kept an eye on us and contacted the fire department when she saw smoke billowing from the shed and garage. The fire truck was "Johnny on the spot," and the damage was minimal.

Due to our young age, my sister, cousin, and I were forgiven and had our hot dogs in the house that night for supper.

My mother was forever grateful to Viola for saving the shed, garage, and family car. There were benefits to growing up in a small town. We watched out for each other. I no longer eat hot dogs.

I'm with my sister Cheryl and behind us is the shed/garage that housed Tip's dog house.

My sister Cheryl is in the drivers seat and directly behind her is my cousin LeJean.

**Learning New Words:** One Halloween my youngest sister, one of our friends, and I went trick or treating. Our friend, Stevie, was the middle son of our new-to-town Methodist preacher. He and his family lived across the alley from our house in the parsonage next door to the church. I was eight-years-old on that Halloween, the oldest in the group, and therefore I felt responsible for the safety of the others. After two hours of trick or treating, we each had a large grocery sack full of candy. On our way home, we were confronted by the preacher's oldest son, Buddy, who was 12-years-old and a bully. He stole all of our candy. We immediately ran home, crying all the way, to tell my mother. She was furious, and she went in search of Buddy with the three of us hot on her heels.

She found him, retrieved our candy, and cussed Buddy out. I didn't know she knew such words, some that I had never heard. She held on to Buddy's arm and we all proceeded to walk the couple of blocks to the parsonage. When my mother rang the doorbell she was still furious, and she continued to use the offensive words in front of the preacher. He was so mad at Buddy that he didn't seem to notice my mother's salty language. Perhaps he knew better than to mess with a mad mama bear.

The next Sunday my mother put on a nice dress, her gloves, her favorite hat, held her head high, and crossed the alley to the Methodist church where she sat in her usual seat on the pew in the last row.

The preacher never mentioned the incident, Buddy never bothered us again, and I learned several new words that Halloween night.

Above: I'm pictured on the left in a Howdy Doody mask that I cut out from the back of a cereal box.

**Not My Monkey:** As a child I had many pets. I had dogs, cats, a pony, mallard ducks, geese, pigeons, hamsters, turtles, and a rabbit. I also had aquariums, and I had parakeets.

The one pet that I desperately wanted was a monkey. I would see ads for squirrel monkeys in the back of comic books. No matter how much I begged my parents to let me order one, the answer was always "No, monkeys are too nasty."

In the fall during cotton harvest when folks had money, there was an auction held each Saturday night in downtown Marmaduke. The auction gave folks an opportunity to socialize and to spend some of their "cotton pickin' money." I loved going to the auctions to watch people bid, and I liked viewing the ever-changing merchandise. At one of the auctions, there was a live monkey that was going up for bid. I arrived at the auction early, saw the monkey, and immediately ran the couple of blocks back home to get my Daddy. I wanted him to go to the auction and bid on the monkey.

He did go back to the auction with me, but he refused to bid on the monkey. Hoping to appease me, he bid on, and bought for me a fairly good sized chalk deer complete with antlers. That helped a little, but it wasn't a monkey. Almost sixty years later, I still have the chalk deer. It has an aged patina, the antlers are long gone, and I've had to glue one of its ears back on a couple of times. Every time I look at the deer, I think, "You should have been a monkey."

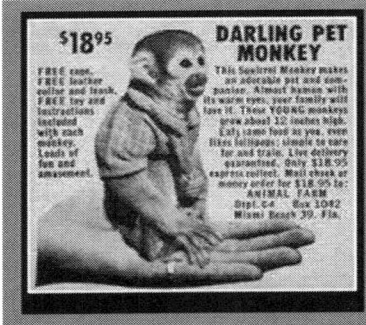 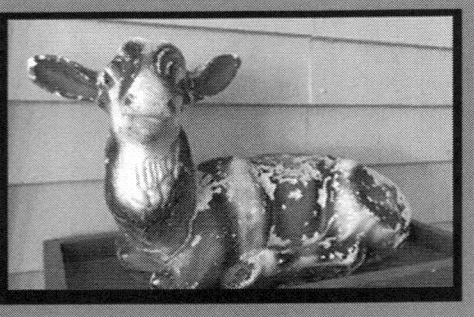

**Fowl Play:** Some of my favorite pets were feathered friends. The first feathered pet that I remember was a black and white speckled hen. She was a gift to me from my first grade teacher, Miss Versa Butler. I named the chicken "polka dot." She lived a long time running around our large yard and sleeping at night in a nesting box in the garage. She fit in just fine with my menagerie, and she seemed to enjoy the company of the other animals including my cats. Eventually she was joined by six ducks and some geese.

My ducks were mallards, two drakes and four hens. Mallard drakes are commonly known as "greenheads," and the hens are called "suzies."

I thought it odd that all the girls had the same name. My daddy brought them home to me when they were ducklings. They were sweet, fuzzy, yellow and brown babies. Until they got feathers, they lived in a cardboard box in my bedroom with a lightbulb hanging above them for warmth. When they were big enough, they moved to the yard, and they never strayed off our property. I never saw them fly. I don't think they realized that they could take to the air. My daddy's bird dog was very protective of the ducks and kept any and all predators at bay. Our house was on concrete pillars and the ducks slept under the house at night. Every now and then, one of the suzies would make a nest and sit on eggs. The eggs never hatched. My daddy said it was because it thundered and prevented the eggs from hatching. I never understood why he thought that could be the reason.

I also had parakeets. Except for one, I named each of them "Timmy" after my favorite TV star, the young boy on "Lassie." The one exception was a solid white keet that I named "Angel." Angel enjoyed riding on top of the cars on my electric train. My oldest sister was terrified of birds. Although it was very naughty of me, I thought it was fun to hear her scream when I would let one of my parakeets fly free in the house. My parents didn't think it was funny. I couldn't help myself.

For several years, I had a large walk-in coop that housed several fantail pigeons. My Uncle Buster gave them to me. Unfortunately, he tagged the ones that were to be mine with rubber bands on one of their legs. He left the bands on too long and by the time I got them, two of the birds had lost a foot. It didn't bother me. I called them my pirate pigeons.

Two of my favorite feathered pets were geese. Early one spring I walked down to the feed store and purchased a pair of goslings. My mother allowed me to keep them. The geese, Mutt and Jeff, quickly imprinted with me and considered me to be their mother. I enjoyed walking the couple of blocks to our downtown with the goslings following me in single file. The goslings would often leave a mess on the sidewalk. It didn't matter much as there were always messes on the sidewalk left by the old men sitting on benches and spitting tobacco. During warm weather, I was always barefoot. When I walked downtown during the summer, I kept my eyes focused on the sidewalks to avoid stepping in the tobacco juice. The summer that I had the goslings, they instinctively weaved through the obstacle course with me.

When the goslings became grown geese, they became territorial. They patrolled our unfenced yard and kept away every creature that they thought didn't belong on the property. Unfortunately that included the women that were coming to my mother's beauty shop. Mutt and Jeff would nip at the ladies' legs and chase them to the door of the shop. My mother said, "They have to go." One of my father's good friends had a cotton patch, and he used geese to weed the cotton. Geese do not like the taste of cotton, but they will eat young Bermuda grass, Johnson grass, sedge and nut grass, puncture vine, clover, chickweed, horsetail and many other weeds. Even though I was sad to see them go, I thought that the cotton farm would be a good place for them to live. I knew they wouldn't be eaten because they would provide a valuable service as weed eaters in the cotton field. The first night that they were gone, I cried while worrying that they were "missing their mother."

Children do not always look like their mother. Not at all.

Fowl Play:
Upper left, I'm in pigeon coop with my youngest sister.
Upper right, some of my ducks in the yard.
Lower left, one of my fantail pigeons.
Lower right, goslings.

**Caw of The Wild:** When I was a child in the Arkansas Delta, I spent as much time outdoors as possible. I loved our large yard in the middle of town, and I enjoyed watching visiting birds that feasted on the fruit from my mother's cherry tree and the grapes from her vines.

I was twelve-years old when I was surprised and delighted by a feathered visitor who showed up in the backyard. It was early spring that year when I went outside and shortly after exiting the screen door, I was startled when a crow landed on my shoulder. Although I flinched, the crow stayed put. I reached up with my hand and gently placed the large bird onto my forearm. The tame crow obviously had been someone's pet.

During the summer that year, nearly every time that I went out the back door, the crow was there to greet me. I had snacks for him from my mother's icebox. He loved bologna. I named him Benny.

Benny would land on my shoulder, my head, or my arm. He did not do the same for other members of my family. The crow and I had a special bond. A few times, the brave bird perched on my shoulder while I rode my pony. There were moments when I thought about taking Ben inside my house and putting him in a cage. I just could not do it. I realized that it was important for him to be free.

In the fall of that year, Benny's visits became fewer, and eventually he quit coming. I was sad, but I hoped that he was safe and sound, and happy. Most of all, I hoped he was still flying free.

Since that time, I've had a fondness for crows, and I often use them as subject matter in my paintings.

Thank you Benny for the inspiration.

**No Need For Shoes**: In Marmaduke, Arkansas, during the '50s and '60s, school was not in session during September and October. Those were the months of cotton harvest, and we were in the fields "a pickin." Instead, we went to school in July and August. During the summer months students attended school in buildings that were not air conditioned. It was hot. The high school did have high ceilings that allowed heat to rise, and the classrooms had large windows for ventilation. Industrial size floor fans ran constantly blowing hot air. The fans created noise that made hearing difficult. We started school at 7 a.m. during the summer months, and our school day would end at 1 p.m. Homes back then weren't air conditioned. It didn't matter that we were hot at school. We would have been hot wherever we were during Delta summers. Due to the heat, school dress codes were fairly lax. Boys were allowed to wear shorts. Girls could not. However, girls could wear "knee knockers," pants that came to the middle of the knee. I often wondered what was so provocative about a girl's leg above the knee that required that area of the anatomy to be covered.

We did have the option to go to class barefoot. Students in the first three grades were required to have a note from home saying it was permissible to be barefoot. A note was not required to be shoeless for students in grades four through twelve.

I loved to be barefoot and that's how I went to school during the summer. I started toughening up my feet as early as possible, and if weather permitted, as early as March. One of my childhood friends had to abide by his mother's rule, "No bare feet before May 1st." I felt a guilty pleasure when I pranced around without shoes in front of him prior to his permissible barefoot date. By May, my feet were very tough. I enjoyed showing off, and I would ask friends to "Watch me run down a gravel road without shoes." The soles of my feet were like leather.

During the warm months there were two requirements at bedtime: check for mosquitoes in the house and wash feet before getting into bed. By bedtime, my feet were black with dirt and required vigorous scrubbing.

There were hazards to being shoeless. While walking downtown to the drug store for a fountain drink, I had to carefully dodge tobacco juice on sidewalks. The brown spit came from the old men sitting on benches in front of the stores. The greatest peril of being barefoot was stepping on honeybees that were feasting on clover. Our yard was filled with the blooms, and I often stepped on a bee. Most of the time the pain was bearable, but it hurt enough that if my parents were in earshot, I would get in trouble for yelling out a cuss word. One spring I was stung multiple times, and I had a very swollen foot that required me to use a cane for a week or two. Whenever I did get a bee sting, if my grandmother was around, she would chew tobacco from one of my daddy's torn up cigarettes. She would make a tobacco poultice, and apply it to the sting to draw out the poison.

The worst barefoot trauma did not happen to me but to my younger sister. When I was eleven-years-old and she was nine, we were bicycling shoeless one night. Her foot on the bike pedal, went up under a car bumper. The bumper almost cut off four of her toes. When I saw what had happened, and for the first time in my life, I fainted. Fortunately, doctors were able to reattach her toes. Although we still went barefoot, we never again rode our bikes without shoes.

I am still a proud barefoot Arkie. No matter the season, when I walk into my house, I immediately kick off my shoes. No need to wait 'til May.

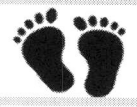

Above: Marmaduke High, Circa 1915

Above Center: Riding my little horse bareback while barefoot

Right: I would mow the lawn while barefoot, perhaps not the smartest thing to do.

**Building Castles:** Fried fish is a staple food in the Arkansas Delta. My family had fish on the table three or four times a month. My daddy ran nets on the Saint Francis River, a swampy river that fed into the Mississippi. He would check the nets every weekend, and many times he brought home a 100-plus pound catfish.

We considered catfish to be fine eatin'. A fish meal would always include fried potatoes, slaw, onion, and hush puppies. When my daddy caught a really big catfish, he would cook it in a big iron kettle in the yard, and everyone in the neighborhood would enjoy the feast.

My family would often go fishing on a Sunday afternoon during the summer. My daddy had a flat bottom boat, olive green in color, and it was powered with an outboard Evinrude motor. The boat was big enough to accommodate my parents, my grandmother, my two sisters, and me.

Early on it became evident that there was no way on earth that I was going to bait a hook. A family member, usually one of my sisters, would bait it for me. I thought, "How could they be so mean to those worms?" When my bait was hooked and in the water, I was bored to death sitting still, holding the bamboo pole, and watching the red and white float while waiting for a bite. I would last about five minutes before I started squirming, talking, and driving everyone crazy. I could not sit still in the boat and be quiet. I was far too fidgety and way too talkative.

When I was ten-years-old, my parents thought that I was capable of taking care of myself, and they thought that it would be best for me, and best for all family members, to leave me on the shore while they went out in the boat. That suited me just fine.

I would spend the afternoons, building castles with the muddy sand, collecting driftwood and mussel shells, catching crawdads and minnows, and exploring. I was a good swimmer. There were no worries about me drowning if I should fall into the river. One would never get in the Saint Francis River on purpose. The water was coffee colored, and the muddy brine was home to water moccasins, snapping turtles, and gar.

At times during the fishing trips, my family would float out of sight and go around a bend in the river. I liked when they couldn't see me. I felt free from supervision, I felt responsible, and I felt grown up. I also felt free to turn cartwheels, dance, sing, and just be silly. I could do whatever I wanted to do without fear of being ridiculed by my sisters.

The fishing trip would end well before dark so there would be enough time to clean the caught fish after we got home. My sisters liked to clean the fish. My daddy had built a fish cleaning table in the backyard.

My sisters, Cheryl and Rhonda, would get the metal hand held grater-like fish scalers, and they would vigorously and rhythmically start removing the scales. No way could I do that. When they slit the fish open to remove whatever was inside, I would gag.

I decided that while they were cleaning the fish, I was better off staying in the house. I would sit in my room, think back about my day, and remember how much fun I had while playing on the riverbank.

I am very fortunate and thankful to have had understanding parents who let me build castles in the sand.

Above left: My grandmother cleaning fish at the cleaning station next to the flat bottom boat.
Above right: I'm pictured with a friend and a large catfish.
Below left: Saint Francis River  Below right: I'm with my sister and cousins and a big fish.

**Let's Pretend:** When I was a child, I spent many hours playing outside and "pretending." I was often joined in playtime by my friends and sisters. In my little Delta town, there were no after school programs or public facilities available to children. We amused ourselves.

I didn't have a playhouse, but when my mother got a new appliance, I turned the large item's shipping container into my own little house. The containers were made of heavy cardboard. I would carefully cut a door and some windows into the box with a butcher knife. I would spend hours drawing on the walls with crayons. I would draw and color curtains around the windows, draw furniture, and create paintings for the walls. On the cardboard floor, I would draw linoleum. After I finished with the decorating, I would spend many hours in the house. My little home was often visited by my youngest sister, my dog Jiggs, and a cat or two. The cardboard playhouses didn't last. They were outside, and they eventually collapsed from getting wet from rainwater.

I did not have a tree house. However, I made a treetop refuge in my backyard by creating a bird's nest. I twined together the honeysuckle vines that were growing in the upper branches in one of our backyard trees. When finished, the bird nest was large enough and strong enough to hold four sixty-pound kids.

I also did not have an elephant. I was a big fan of Johnny Weissmuller's "Tarzan" movies. The films often played late afternoons as one of the 'Million Dollar Movies" broadcast from a Memphis television station. I saw each one several times. I wanted to be Tarzan. I needed an elephant. The closest thing available that I could pretend to be an elephant was the propane tank in our backyard. I spent many an hour riding it. If my little cat "Mitzi" was nearby, she became a ferocious lion.

One time my elephant almost did me in. I was a growing boy and eventually became tall enough to reach the electric wires that were above the propane tank. The lines ran from the house to an out building. One day I decided they were vines, and I should grab them and swing just like Tarzan did in the movies. I jumped up and grabbed the wires. The wires stretched down enough that my bare feet were back on the metal tank. I received a tremendous jolt of electricity. The jolt was 100 times stronger than the shock I had received the time that I had stuck a bobby pin into an electric outlet.

My mother was in the kitchen and heard me screaming. She saw what was happening, ran out with a broom and knocked me off the tank. The electric wires were still in my hand when I hit the ground. They were pulled completely off the house. I was "shook up" from my near fatal jungle ride and I stayed off my elephant . . . for a while. Pretending to be Tarzan, I craved excitement and danger. Imagination sometimes becomes reality.

Above: On the propane tank with electric wires overhead
Below: my grandmother, "Mom," holding Mitzi and Jiggs.

Above: I'm holding my lion, Mitzi.
Below: A little older but still giving the Tarzan yell.

**Jump Down, Turn Around, Pick a Bail of Cotton**: I started picking cotton in 1951 at the age of five. My grandmother, Eva Belle Harvey, had picked cotton all of her life. I loved my grandma, and even if it meant "working in the field," I wanted to do it just to be with her. She made a little cotton pick sack out of a pillowcase for me, and she attached a colorful shoulder strap to it. The sack was just the right size for a little boy.

When I got older, I went to the fields with friends, and I graduated to using much larger pick sacks. The sacks were made of heavy-duty canvas duck with rubber or tar reinforcement on the bottom side to keep them from wearing out as they were being drug on the ground. Sacks were available in six foot, seven foot, and nine foot lengths. Pickers placed a rock or cotton boll in one of the inside corners of the sack at the bottom, and secured it with a wire made into a loop on the exterior. The wire loop allowed for the cotton filled sack to be hung on a scale and weighed.

At the beginning of the season, the cotton husks were hard on the hands. Some pickers wore cotton jersey gloves with the ends of the fingers cut from the gloves. I picked bare handed. It didn't take long for my fingers to toughen and become calloused.

When poke berries were ripe, we would decorate our sacks with the bright purple juice from the berries. We would draw pictures on the sacks, and write our names on them. That was our form of graffiti.

Cotton farmers didn't want to pay for wet cotton. It weighed more at the scales. Therefore, workdays in the cotton patch started the minute the dew was off the plants. We were paid three cents a pound, three dollars a hundred. Older pickers would work two rows at a time, one on each side. It was grueling backbreaking work. We would alternate between bending over and crawling along on our knees while we picked. Tall cotton not only yielded more but also meant a person didn't have to work as hard because they didn't have to bend over so far. In the south the term "Walking in tall cotton," also means "times are good and a person is successful."

When a pick sack was filled, it was hoisted across the picker's shoulder and carried to the cotton wagon to be weighed and emptied. Lifting that filled sack was at times the hardest task of the day. A nine foot sack could hold 70 pounds or more. Emptying the sack in the cotton wagon was also difficult. At each weighing, the farmer would record the pounds picked by each worker. He would use a pencil to write the numbers down in a notebook. Even though I was a scrawny teen weighing about 110 pounds, I could pick between three and four hundred pounds of cotton a day. We were paid in cash at the end of each workday.

Pickers would break for lunch midday, find shade, and eat with dirty hands. Each worker brought their own lunch. We called the noon meal "dinner." It usually consisted of sandwiches, chips, or the ever-popular canned Vienna sausage. Oftentimes my mother would make me a sandwich from left over breakfast sausage and biscuit wrapped in tin foil. In the heat, the sausage and biscuit sandwich would stay nice and warm.

If the cotton farmer had crushed ice available in a tub, we were able to keep our coca colas nice and cold. We also kept our drinks cooled in thermos bottles. The cotton farmers did have cold water available for drinking that was cooled by a big chunk of ice. We all shared one metal long handled dipper to drink from, and no one thought anything about sharing that dipper.

Fields were picked three times. Workers preferred fields that offered "first picking" because the yield was higher. When the fields were picked the second time through, there was less cotton to harvest. By the time of the last picking, the third time through, there wasn't much left and most of the cotton bolls were rotten That picking was called "pulling." When we "pulled cotton," we could strip the stalk and put the cotton along with the attached hulls into the sack.

For the first and second pickings, the cotton farmers wanted the cotton to be clean with no trash in the pick sack. Because trashy cotton weighed more, when we pulled, we received only two cents a pound. I could pull about 400 pounds a day. Pulling was done late fall and often it was chilly and we worked while wearing flannel shirts.

I liked working in the fields and making money. I used my "cotton picking" money to buy school clothes, books, and school supplies. I also made enough money at the age of twelve to buy a small horse. At the age of fourteen with my cotton pickin' money, I purchased a small Allstate motorcycle for $125 from the Sears catalogue. At the age of 16, I was able to buy a '52 Ford for $300. I continued picking cotton each fall until I graduated from high school at the age of seventeen.

Back then I thought life was good and that I was truly "walking in tall cotton." I am grateful for my early work experience. It taught me "incentive." I learned that the harder that I worked and applied myself, the greater the rewards. It was a valuable lesson that I still try to apply to my life today. I'm still "walking in tall cotton."

**No, I Don't Speak Spanish, Yes:** During the '50s and '60s, cotton harvests in the fall brought interesting visitors to my little Arkansas Delta town. One of the local cotton growers who farmed hundreds of acres, brought in migrant pickers from Mexico. The cotton farmer owned a couple of old school buses that transported the workers from South of the Border to Arkansas to work during the eight weeks of harvest.

The Mexicans, all men, worked for lower wages than we did. They picked for two cents a pound, two dollars for a hundred pounds. We were getting three cents a pound, and that equaled three dollars a hundred pounds. The Mexican pickers were extremely hard workers. Often on the way to work, I would pass by a field where they were working. I could see from the amount of cotton in their sacks, they had been picking since daybreak. The only thing that could delay an early start would be a heavy dew. Farmers wouldn't let workers start until the dew lifted. The moisture would have increased the weight of the cotton when weighed at the scales.

The Mexican workers had a different method of picking than we did. We would drag our pick sacks draped across one shoulder and we picked to the side. Many of the pickers from Mexico would straddle their pick sacks and drag the heavy bags of cotton between their legs.

## Out of the Delta

The Mexicans lived in shotgun shacks on the cotton farm. Housing was provided by the cotton grower. Ten or more men would live in one of the two bedroom houses. The houses were called shotgun shacks because they were long and narrow with one room directly behind the next. The doors were lined up in such a way that it was said you could shoot a shotgun through the front door, and the shot would travel all the way through the house and out the back door. Most of the shacks were without indoor plumbing, and had hand drawn wells and outhouses.

When I was a child I was curious about the workers from another country. They were very different from the folks living in my area. After working in the fields all week, the Mexicans enjoyed coming into town on Saturday nights. They ate in the local cafes, and they bought food in the grocery stores to take back to their shotgun shack homes.

When I was around ten I befriended one of the workers, Juan. I sought him out every Saturday night during the fall of that year when the workers came into town. Juan was in his twenties. Despite our language barrier we had a good time together. Juan taught me words in Spanish and I taught him some English words. He would point to an object and I would tell him the word for it in English, and he likewise would tell me the word in Spanish.

On the last Saturday spent with Juan before he was to go home to Mexico, we continued our language lessons. Juan pointed to a piece of wood that was placed across a ditch as a walkway. I said, "Plank, it's a plank." He told me the Spanish word.

After he had left that evening, I worried almost to the point of obsessing that I should have said "board" instead of "plank." I worried about my conceived mistake for weeks. I hoped that Juan would return for the next cotton harvest so that I could make the needed correction.

I never saw him again. However, I doubt if he remembered the English word "plank" any more than I remember the Spanish word for the object. I still don't know.

Shotgun shack                          Cotton in the field

**Little Zeek Wanted a Pony:** One of my favorite childhood books was "Little Benny Wanted a Pony." After reading the book, I too wanted a pony. When I was twelve-years-old, my parents said that if I made enough money picking cotton to purchase a pony, then I could have one. From the minute they told me that, I couldn't wait for cotton picking season to begin.

I didn't want just any pony, I wanted a pinto. I had Native American blood in my heritage from both of my maternal grandparents. From watching westerns on television, I came to the conclusion that most Indians had pintos. I would settle for no less. I felt that it was my obligation to ride a multi-colored horse in honor of my heritage.

A few weeks before the cotton season, my daddy and I made plans to build a stable and to fence the very large lot next to our house. We were in the middle of a little Delta town, and there were no zoning restrictions concerning livestock and fowl. A friend of mine in town had a cow that he rode on occasion, and many folks inside the city limits had chicken pens. Bunk Tuberville who lived in town, had a team of horses, a white one named Buttermilk and a red one named Lipstick. Bunk used the team for plowing gardens for "pretty near" everyone in town. Humans and beasts lived in harmony in Marmaduke.

Daddy could see how determined I was to buy a pony, and he knew that we should have the stable and fence ready before the beginning of the cotton harvest. We worked together to build the stable, and we enjoyed working together. However, at times he did get tired of my constant babbling about my future equine purchase.

My great uncle Floyd was a wheeler dealer and a gambler. He always had odds and ends to sell, including merchandise that he won while playing cards. About that time he won a small pinto gelding in a poker game. It was larger than a Shetland, but not as big as most horses. It was the perfect size for a twelve-year-old, and it was a pinto. He offered to sell the small horse to me complete with saddle for $125. He said that he would hold it for me until I could come up with the money.

I quickly estimated that at three cents for picking a pound of cotton, I would need to pick over 4,200 pounds of cotton in two months. I had to average picking 525 pounds a week. When I was twelve-years-old, I could pick between 125 to 150 pounds a day. I was confident that I could reach my goal during the eight weeks of harvest. I did and I got my little horse. I even made some extra money, enough to buy a curry comb, and other accessories necessary for equine care.

The little horse's name was Prince. I didn't like the name very much, but I was advised to keep it. I did keep the name, but I added "Albert." "Prince Albert" was the name of a popular pipe tobacco. What I didn't know when I purchased him, is that Prince hadn't been broke. I tried to ride him, but being inexperienced, I kept getting bucked off. My parents were proud of the hard work I had put in that fall while picking cotton. They decided to reward me by paying to have Prince trained by a professional. When he came back to me from the horse trainer, Prince was rideable.

Despite being trained by the pro, the horse still had a stubborn streak. It was a constant struggle between us as to who was the boss. I could handle him most of the time. However, he was always kicking and leaving bruises on my sister and my friends. He bucked one of my friends off of him, and that friend suffered a broken arm. If I had the saddle on Prince, even when he bucked, I could stay astride. If I was on him bareback, I was thrown off. Sometimes when he decided he didn't want me on him, he would lie down and roll over. I had no choice but to get off of him.

Although we were often at odds as to who was the "master," Prince Albert and I did love and respect each other. I think we understood each other. I was stubborn myself. I also knew that he would do anything I wanted him to do if I kept apples handy as treats. I enjoyed that wonderful creature for the many years that I had him. He was worth every pound of cotton that I picked to purchase him.

Hard work paid off and I still love the smell of a horse.

One small horse equals 4,200 pounds of cotton.

Zeek Taylor

## 2 HAPPY TIMES IN HAPPY TOWN

**Turtles and Toilet Paper:** When I was a kid, a goodly number of houses in the little town where I lived did not have indoor plumbing. Those homes had outhouses in the backyards. The two churches that were across the alley from my family home had outhouses that received a great deal of use. My grandmother's house on the edge of town did not have indoor plumbing. When I visited her, I used the outhouse. It was not a pleasant experience sitting on a hard wooden seat. One had to be vigilant about wasps in the outhouses during warm weather. Using one during cold weather was almost painful. Unlike most areas, we called outhouses "toilets," and the porcelain thing indoors was called a "commode."

My family home did have indoor plumbing. My parents put in a bathroom when they bought their home in the 1940s. They did leave the outhouse in the backyard to be used as our second bathroom. Because I had two sisters who seemed to always be in the indoor bathroom, our outhouse often came in handy for me to use.

Marmaduke did not have a sewer system. When a toilet was flushed, it ran through pipes and emptied into one of a series of tunnels and into open ditches that crisscrossed the town. Citizens of the town were not allowed to flush toilet paper. The paper was placed in a covered trash can. In hot weather the smell from the ditches was unpleasant. Mosquito larvae could be seen wiggling in the stinky grey water.

Snapping turtles, some bigger than dinner plates, lived in the ditches. At times they would venture into our yard. I thought they were interesting creatures akin to dinosaurs. I did find them a little scary, but like most kids, I liked being scared. When a snapping turtle crawled out of a ditch, I enticed it to bite down on a stick, a natural instinct for the snapper. The turtle would not let go, and I would carry it and the stick back to the ditch. I had heard that when they did bite, they would not let go until it thundered. I was somewhat disappointed when I found it to not be true.

The ditches were fairly deep and ran under the streets through three foot wide rectangular concrete culverts. As a kid, I thought it was fun to get in the tunnel, legs and arms splayed outward, and monkey walk through the tunnel under the street with my body well above the sewage. That "fun" did come to an end one day.

My Great-aunt Beulah who lived in Detroit, had sent me a flannel shirt for my birthday. It was cream, brown, and green colored, and was patterned with figures of cowboys riding bucking broncos. I loved the shirt. One day while wearing it, I straddled the tunnel under the street. As usual I was very proud of my athletic skill as I made my way through the tunnel just two feet above the putrid water. My foot slipped and down I went. My favorite shirt was covered with nasty sewage. I ran to the house crying. My mother made me go to the back porch and undress. She had planned to throw away all my clothes, but after much begging on my part, she saved my flannel shirt. She washed it several times before she let me wear it again. I continued to rescue snapping turtles, but I never again ventured into the tunnel.

When I was in my early teens, my father was elected mayor of our town. He was responsible for getting a modern sewer system installed. The smell went away, and the snapping turtles moved on. I did miss the turtles.

Above left: Snapping Turtle
Right: Zeek, the tunnel walker

**Turkey Day, Duck Day:** I was born on Thanksgiving Day. My Father joked that he was mad at me from the very beginning because "I knocked him out of a day off." He worked in a bank and he would have been off on Thanksgiving Day. He also would have been allowed to take a day off the day I was born to transport my mother to the hospital, and be present for my birth. Due to my arrival date, both days off were combined into one.

I think the real reason that he was mad at me for being born on that day, was that I knocked him out of a duck hunt. The first day of duck hunting season was Thanksgiving Day. On opening day, he would get up long before daybreak and go to his duck blind on the Saint Francis River.

The river was located in the Mississippi River Flyway, a migratory route for mallards and other species of ducks. The Saint Francis was about five miles from our house. It was a swampy river filled with cypress trees, and water moccasins. It was a nighttime resting place for the migrating waterfowl. Daddy always hunted duck on Thanksgiving morning, but he would make it back home in plenty of time for the midday holiday meal.

When I was ten-years-old, I was invited to go with him to duck hunt on opening day. Daddy woke me up at 3:30 a.m. I quickly dressed, and climbed into his '39 Chevy, a black car that he had named Ol' Betsy. The car had a removable rack on top that held a flat bottom boat that we were to take on our water journey to the duck blind. As we neared the Saint

Francis levee, we stopped at a sharecropper's shotgun shack where we picked up my father's best friend, Lonzo. The minute Lonzo got into the car, the two men started drinking Old Crow whiskey. A few minutes later we were at the river. We took a fifteen minute boat ride in the dark through swampy passages. As a ten-year-old boy, I found the ride exhilarating and very scary. I had heard tales of snakes falling out of trees into boats and I was fearfully thinking about the 15-foot-long water moccasin that, according to legend, lived in the Saint Francis River.

Below: Daddy with ducks and the Saint Francis River.

The duck blind was a very small wooden shack, and it sat on stilts in the water. We exited the boat, and climbed up the ladder into the blind. It was very cold, but the blind was soon warmed by a small fire built in a charcoal bucket. A galvanized coffee pot was placed on the blazing charcoal, and soon the air was filled with the smell of strong chicory coffee.

I drank the coffee from a metal cup. The two grown-ups drank the coffee and chased each sip with Old Crow. I was too young for whiskey and too afraid to ask for a swig, even though I had sampled my daddy's whiskey numerous times unbeknownst to him. We sat and we waited. Just before dawn, I was told to be very quiet. As daylight crept in, we could hear ducks quacking. My father and his friend were poised at a window opening in the blind, guns in place, as they waited for the ducks to fly over. All of a sudden, dozens flew over, and shots were fired. No ducks were hit. I think all the whiskey might have affected the men's ability to aim properly.

We didn't see another duck. I was bored, chilly, and tired of drinking the strong bitter coffee. On the way home, I slept in the car. Daddy shook me awake when we got home. I was very happy to enter my warm home, see my mother, and join my family for the Thanksgiving feast.

That was the one and only time that I went duck hunting. Although I loved my daddy, I knew that hunting was not my thing. Thereafter, I spent my Thanksgiving mornings at home with my mother, safe from snakes, and watching the Macy's Thanksgiving Parade.

**I Almost Saw Kim Novak:** In the small Delta town where I grew up there was a movie theater that seated less than 100 people. For a town with a population of 650 that was plenty large enough. For a special end-of-school year treat, the town's elementary students were bused to the theater for a showing of "Black Beauty." The feature film was the same each year, and it was preceded by a Little Rascals short film, "The Kid from Borneo." The short featured a crazed jungle native chasing the rascal kids while yelling, "Yum, yum, eat em' up!" It was both scary and funny.

The main attraction, "Black Beauty," was about a horse, and the movie was wrought with drama and suspense. Fortunately for the young audience, the movie had a happy ending. I only got to attend the special showing two or three times before the theater closed.

A large fancy movie house, the Capitol Theater, was ten miles down the road. The screen was much larger than the one that had been in my hometown's little theater. The seats were very plush. When Elvis started making movies, the Capitol Theater would premiere his holiday release on Thanksgiving afternoons. We always attended that premiere. Following a midday holiday dinner, my father would drive the family to the theater, let us off, and he would be waiting to pick us up after the movie ended. With the exception of seeing "Gone With the Wind," my father never attended an indoor movie.

However, he did see films when he took our family to the Sunset drive-in movie in nearby Paragould. I think he was willing to go to the drive-in because he could take a bottle of whiskey to sip on. My mother made snacks for us to munch. However, as kids we also wanted to go to the concession stand for popcorn, cokes, and big dill pickles.

I loved the movies, but even more I enjoyed playing on the playground that was set up in front of the movie screen. The minute the car stopped, my sisters and I would make a beeline for the playground knowing that we had a limited time to play before the movie started. We liked to whirl around on the spinning disc we called a merry-go-round. During the hot summer months, the car windows had to remain down. My father would buy a citronella incense swirled repellant. When lit, it kept the mosquitoes at bay. On the 4th of July there was a special fireworks display between the double features at the Sunset Drive-in.

As a teen, I continued going to the drive-in with my friends. One weekend there was a scheduled showing of a double feature of Kim Novak movies. She was a very popular actress at the time. The owner of the drive-in ran ads in the local paper that said Kim Novak would be there and would make a special appearance between the two movies. I was very excited as I had not seen anyone famous. My friends and I arrived very early and got in a long line of cars. Soon the drive-in was filled to capacity. We anxiously awaited the end of the first feature and the appearance of Miss Novak.

After the first movie ended, most folks left their cars and headed for the concession stand where the star was to make her appearance on the roof

The owner of the drive-in appeared on the roof. He was accompanied by his young daughter. His last name was Novak and his daughter's name was Kim. The crowd went berserk when they realized the little girl was the "Kim Novak" that had been advertised to appear. I feared that the man and the kid were not going to get off the roof alive.

People were screaming and yelling while throwing wadded up paper cups and popcorn boxes at the two Novaks. Folks got back into their cars and started honking their car horns. Everyone was mad as hell, and several cars peeled out. Quite a few speakers were torn from metal poles. Many of the movie goers demanded refunds as they exited.

I learned one thing that night: If you promise folks Kim Novak, then it better be Kim Novak. The "real" Kim Novak.
Whatever you promise, it is best to deliver.

**Above: Sunset Drive-in movie**  **Above: Capitol Theater, Paragould, AR**

**Lucky in the Danger Zone:** I did things as a child that today would be thought unwise to do, and perhaps some of the activities would even be banned. Often those choices involved the chewing and digesting of unsavory or toxic items. I loved the miniature wax soda bottles sold as candy and filled with colored fruit flavored liquid. Although I don't think toxins were involved, it made little nutritional sense to bite off the bottle top, drink the liquid, and then spend hours chewing the wax. It was a cheap treat. The cost of a package of five of the little bottles was a nickel.

A worse chewing choice was the plastic bubbles that I blew with a tiny plastic straw. The plastic was squeezed as a gooey liquid from a tube, and placed on the end of the straw. The goop was turned into a bubble by blowing through the straw. The bubble lasted for a while, but when it deflated, I chewed the plastic. I enjoyed the chemical taste and the tough texture that made chewing a challenge. I would chew until my jaw gave out.

During the spring, my friends and I enjoyed eating sheepshire from the yard. The plant was light green, looked like small clover, and had a yellow bloom. The plant had a sour bitter taste. I didn't like it, but I ate it just because I could. Later I learned that it was a type of oxalis and was toxic if digested in large quantities. Apparently I never ate that much because I never did get ill.

Some activities that were possibly harmful involved inhaling smoke and fumes. My mother had a grape arbor in our backyard and it supplied me with an ample supply of dried grapevines to secretly smoke. I coughed with each drag and my lungs ached.

I enjoyed following the mosquito fogging truck that drove through town during evenings in the summer. It was like playing in the clouds. I also spent many hours as a teen sitting in a car at the drive-in movie with a Pic mosquito coil burning. Later studies warned that prolonged exposure to Pic could be harmful.

Top left: wax soda bottles
Top middle: Sheepshire
Top right: pic mosquito repellent coil
Left: Zeek as survivor
Bottom left: plastic bubbles
Bottom right: foot x-ray machine

Every Saturday my family would go to Paragould, Arkansas, to shop for groceries. While in Paragould, my sister and I would often run down to the Red Goose shoe store to view our feet through the store's foot x-ray machine. It was fun to wiggle our toes while seeing the bones in our feet. We had no idea that over exposure to x-rays could be harmful.

My friends and I also enjoyed playing with mercury. It is the only metal that is liquid at room temperature. We would use the element to shine coins while being careful not to let the mercury separate into lots of little balls that scattered everywhere. We didn't know that it was very toxic.

While unaware that some of our childhood activities were harmful, there were things we avoided or did cautiously because we were warned by adults that they were harmful. They weren't. We would worry that if we crossed our eyes, they would stay that way. We were warned against swallowing a watermelon seed because a watermelon would grow in our stomach. We believed that if we caught a toad, and it peed on our hand, we would get warts. Although I was told not to do so, I would throw caution to the wind and hang upside down from the monkey bars even though I had been warned that my liver would turn over. As far as I know, it did not.

In spite of unknown and even untrue hazards, most folks my age survived childhood and seem to be no worse for wear. "What doesn't kill you, makes you stronger …… sometimes …... but sometimes it kills you." Just lucky I guess.

**Doctored:** While growing up in the Arkansas Delta, I knew many people, including family members, who practiced alternate forms of medicine based on old time cures and folklore.

If I had a cold, my mother would plaster my neck and chest with Vicks VapoRub, and she would wrap one of my daddy's long wool socks around my neck. The sock was very scratchy. It was worth the discomfort that followed the soothing touch of my mother's hands when she rubbed the Vicks onto my chest and neck. The Vicks treatment was accompanied with several doses of hot toddy: hot water, sugar, lemon, and whiskey all mixed together. For many years, I associated whiskey with medicine. A cure for a sore throat that my mother used was a warm salt water gargle. I still do that today when my throat is sore.

I never did have a tetanus shot as a child. My grandmother knew what to do to prevent tetanus and other infections when a wound occurred. If the weather was warm, I was barefoot. I was constantly cutting my feet or stepping on rusty nails. When that happened, my grandmother would pour coal oil into a big enameled metal pan, and I would soak my hurt foot in the coal oil for several minutes. Not once did my foot get infected from a cut or puncture. Another hazard to being barefoot was stepping on honeybees that dined on the clover in our yard. Every week or so, I would step on a bee and get a bad sting. My grandmother would remove the tobacco from one of my daddy's Camel cigarettes and, she would chew it until it was a paste. She applied the paste to the swollen spot on my foot. She said "It draws out the poison." If one of my daddy's cigarettes wasn't available, she used baking soda that she had mixed with water to make a healing paste.

My mother and her friends eased the pain of arthritis by swallowing a poke berry every morning. They gathered the berries, washed them, and put a year's supply of 365 berries into the freezer. Even though the seeds of the berries are thought to be toxic, the women never seemed to suffer ill effects, and they swore that the berries eased their pain. Poke berries and juice from the poke plant has been used for centuries, not only by early settlers, but by Native Americans who used the berries to treat any number of ailments. Scientists have studied and are still studying the medicinal uses of the poke plant. The women who swallowed the berries may have been on to something that really did lessen their aches.

Although I think there was validity to some of the folk cures that were used in the Delta, some applications made little sense or offered a logical explanation. There were two or three people in my town who were known to cure colic by blowing into a baby's mouth. The qualification of a person who could cure colic was to be one who had never seen his or her father. Mothers would call on these folks to cure babies of this common malady.

**Above left: cure for bee sting**
**Above center: easing medicine for arthritis**
**Above right: cure for colds (just add hot toddy.)**

**Below left: chicken pox cure**
**Below right: I'm pictured with my grandmother, my mother and my grandmother's dog Ol' Bullet.**

We mistakenly thought that toads caused warts. If one of the hoppy creatures urinated on a person, we believed that the person was destined to get a wart. I played with toads, but I was very careful to avoid their pee. For those that did get a wart, they visited Mr. Parish who could cure them of the unsightly blemish. Mr. Parish would rub the wart with a rag, say something under his breath, and then tell the afflicted to bury the rag in their yard. The wart would disappear within a week. As unlikely as that wart removal method sounds, I saw it work more than once. I think it was a case of "mind over matter." The belief that the wart would be gone, let the body get rid of it.

The cure that I most question was my grandmother's "sure fire" way to get rid of chicken pox. When I came down with the childhood disease, she took me out to her chicken pen and threw a chicken over my head. I don't believe that cured me, but hey, the pox was gone in a week's time.

Some things in life defy logic, but if those things work, "Accept the gift and go with it."

**Eatin' Good, Eatin' Bad:** My mother and grandmother loved to cook, but neither would have been labeled as gourmet chefs. Both were good ol' southern cooks par excellence. To be a good southern cook one should be able to batter and fry any and all vegetables, collect jello salad recipes, have Velveeta "at the ready," and have a grease can on the stove.

Growing up I ate most anything and everything that was put on my plate including, catfish, turnip, mustard, or collard greens, liver and onions, chocolate gravy with homemade biscuits, and fried bologna.

Although I would eat Vienna sausage straight out of the can and I enjoyed fried Spam with scrambled eggs, there were a few things that I did refuse to eat. When my mother served fried brains for breakfast, I would retreat to the living room with a bowl of oatmeal. I could not look at fried quail because they looked like little cooked birds. I would not eat mountain oysters, gizzards, or tongue, most organs with the exception of liver, and I never did try chitlins.

My father was a duck hunter. My mother would cook the ducks with dressing or smoother the fowl in a very soupy barbecue sauce. The duck when served with dressing was very dark and dry. I did like the barbecued duck. Because of the liquid sauce, it was somewhat moist. When eating the duck, I would chew cautiously and try to not to bite down on metal shots that were scattered throughout the meat.

With the exception of turtle doves, my grandmother would eat anything. She considered the dove as "the bird of Peace," and she thought that it should never be eaten. However, she cooked and devoured everything else: wild rabbit, squirrel, raccoon, and other game that I refused to eat. She also loved pickled pigs feet.

When my great-grandfather was living, my grandmother would cook a hog's tail in a pot of boiled cabbage. My grandfather loved the hog's tail. I was nauseated by the sight of it, long and pink, and lying on his plate. Even though I loved boiled cabbage, if a hog's tail was cooked with it, I passed.

Two unusual desserts that my grandmother made were vinegar cobbler and green grape cobbler. She told me that when she was growing up that fresh fruit was not often available, and at times canned fruit would not last the winter. Vinegar served as a substitute for fruit. Green unripe grapes were also a good substitute for fruits that didn't ripen until later in the season. I looked forward to visits from my Great-uncle Floyd because I knew my grandmother would make him his favorite dish, a vinegar cobbler. It was delicious with a taste best described as "sweet & sour."

**Above: cornbread and buttermilk**
**Above right: grease can**
**Right: Velveeta, a southern food staple.**

It's not easy for me to pick out a favorite southern dish, but near the top of my list would be cornbread and buttermilk. It too was a favorite food of my mother and grandmother. It is very filling and easy to prepare: crumble cornbread, place in a glass, pour in buttermilk, and eat with a spoon. The cornbread should be prepared southern style, and that means without sugar in the recipe.

Even though I enjoy many kinds of food, both regional and ethnic, I still prefer good ol' southern cooking. It tastes like "home."

**All The Gold Is in California**: While growing up in the Northeast Arkansas Delta, I thought most rich folk lived in California. I also thought that all wealthy people drove Cadillac cars, had palm trees in their yards, used cigarette holders, and owned French poodles who wore rhinestone collars. In the little town where I grew up, if anyone had money, I wasn't aware of it. I never saw anyone walking a poodle in Marmaduke, Arkansas.

With few exceptions, folks in my town did not have money. The upside of that was there was no separation due to class based on finances.

We were all in the same boat, or at least in the same cotton patch. It was not unusual for our homecoming queen to live in a house without indoor plumbing. There was a line of town folk at city hall each month who were getting their government commodities, food supplements that included block cheese, tubs of peanut butter, rice, and beans. No one was looked down upon because they "didn't have," but they were helped and lifted up by those who did have a little more. If anyone in the area did have money, it was probably the owners of fertile farmland east of town. Their fields yielded good crops of soybeans and cotton.

**Above left: Marmaduke cotton gin**

**Center left: cotton, money on a stalk**

**Upper right: Zeek with poodle puppy, Chelsea Brown**

**Bottom left: "pickers" near Marmaduke.**

The dirt in that part of the county was rich black gumbo. Before the area was drained, it had once been swampland. The Northeast Delta has always yielded some of the best cotton crops in the state. If the owners of the land did have money, they didn't make a show of it. Sharecroppers also worked the land. They worked just as hard if not harder than most, but unfortunately they were among the poorest in our community.

The one time of the year when folks in my town had a little disposable cash was during the fall. Most of us picked cotton, and even though we only received three dollars per hundred pounds picked, by week's end, we had some money in our pockets. We were paid daily for our labor.

Each evening after working in the field, I counted my day's income and placed it inside a cigar box that I hid in my sock drawer. I knew it wasn't going to happen, but I sometimes wondered if I had saved enough money for a bus ticket to California.

There were two cotton gins in Marmaduke. During the fall the smell of burning cotton hulls permeated the air. I often heard people say, "Smells like money to me." With money in hand on Saturday night, I along with many other fellow cotton pickers would go to an auction that was held downtown. I enjoyed watching people bidding and buying, while I carefully kept my hand down. I was hoarding my cash for bigger purchases.

At the age of twelve, I bought a small horse. When I turned fourteen I bought a small motorcycle. When I turned sixteen, I used my cotton picking money to buy a '52 Ford for $300. Even though it wasn't a Cadillac, I felt rich because I had wheels of my own.

I'm glad that I grew up the way that I did, and not judging folks according to their financial worth. Even though I thought those rich people in California were glamorous and interesting, I never entertained the thought that they were better. Even though I am comfortable enough, I did not get rich. I did not move to California. However, I did at one time own a poodle. That's close enough.

**Shopping in Memphis:** While growing up in the Arkansas Delta, Memphis was our go-to metro area. Our television stations were broadcast from Memphis, and two daily newspapers, the Memphis Commercial Appeal and the Memphis Press Scimitar, were delivered to our home daily. If we needed to go to a specialist for medical care, we headed to Memphis. Besides going to the Overton Park Zoo in that city, what I remember most about Memphis was shopping downtown.

After crossing the Mississippi River Bridge and arriving in the city, my family would begin their shopping day at the large Sears store on Crossover Road. Sears was "the" place to shop. My younger sister and I liked going there because they had an escalator. While my parents shopped, my sister and I rode the escalator up and down and rode it over and over again.

After we left Sears, we headed for the downtown area of Memphis. My father knew what he wanted to buy and went to two stores, the Thom McAn shoe store and Robert Hall men's store. He finished his shopping in less than an hour, and he spent the rest of the day sitting on a park bench and feeding pigeons in Court Square Park.

At noon, Daddy would join the family for lunch at the Piccadilly Cafeteria. Before entering the cafeteria, he would always advise, "Don't let your eyes be bigger than your stomach." The advice fell on deaf ears as my younger sister and I loaded up our trays. We were particularly fond of the shrimp cocktail that was served in a lovely glass with a tiny sterling silver cocktail fork. I enjoyed watching the young men employees who wore white jackets and white gloves. They balanced several trays of food that they carried to the tables. When very young, I thought, "That's what I want to do when I grow up, wear an elegant white jacket and white gloves, and juggle trays at the Piccadilly." After we finished lunch, the serious shopping would begin.

My favorite time to shop in Memphis was during the Christmas season. There were two major department stores, Goldsmith's and Lowenstein's, and both were decorated inside and out during the holidays.

Lowenstein's had a special Christmas spokesperson, Mr. Bingle, a snowman puppet who was featured in the store's window. He had his own television show that aired during the month before Christmas. I watched him on TV every day after school during December. I couldn't wait to get to Memphis and to see Mr. Bingle in person in the department store's window.

Christmas shopping in the city also included going to Goldsmith's for a visit with Santa. I would sit on Santa's lap and tell him what I wanted for gifts, ones that I had carefully selected from the Sears Christmas catalogue.

**Mr. Bingle**     **Mr. Bingle Show**     **Court Square, Memphis.**

When I got older, around twelve years of age, I was allowed to run around by myself to shop in downtown Memphis. One of my favorite stores was the young man's clothing store, "The One-Two-Three Shop."

I had a "secret" favorite store, a small newsstand near Court Square. The newsstand sold adult magazines. By today's standards, the adult magazines were very tame. As a teen, I spent quite a bit of time in the newsstand during each trip. The owner didn't seem to mind that I looked through the adult publications.

Around the age of fifteen, I finally got the nerve to buy an adult magazine, smuggled it home, and I hid it under my mattress. After buying the magazine, I volunteered to always change the sheets on my bed.

And I did.

**You Say Potato, and So Do I**: While I was growing up in the Arkansas Delta, the folks who lived there shared a common language that was slow, easy, and often colorful. When I moved from that region, I had to learn different words and expressions in order to fit in, and for everyone to clearly understand just what I was trying to say.

I'm pictured with my grandmother and two sisters. We are wearing "our Sunday go to meeting clothes."

Above: coke, coke, coke, coke, & coke

There was a generational gap when it came to word usage. However, I had heard the "old-timey" words used by the older folks enough that I could interpret their meaning. When my grandmother said "vittles," I knew she meant "food." She called pots and pans "vessels." What she called "ketchup" was a homemade tomato relish, and was something that I would never put on fries.

If she said to "sit pretty," I knew she meant for me to sit down and behave. When my grandmother was going to cook, or to do anything, we knew she was "fixin" to do something. "Fixin" is so embedded in my vocabulary that I still say that word without thinking.

If one was "fixin" to go to "town," that meant they were going shopping. Town for us was 10 miles away and that town was Paragould, Arkansas. On the way to town we would pass by several "mile crossings," a place where a road crossed over the railroad track every mile.

While in town we went to Kroger's, the main grocery store. All paper sacks at my house were known as "Kroger sacks." If we bought a soda pop, it didn't matter if it was a Pepsi, an RC, or another flavor, we were getting a "coke." While in town if we bought manufactured clothes, they were "store-bought," and not "homemade." Potatoes came in burlap bags that we called tow sacks. We called french fries, "fried potatoes." "Commodities" had nothing to do with the stock market. They were food rations that po' folk received in lieu of food stamps.

In the Delta, if folks said they were going to have dinner, then they were going to eat their noon meal. When my daddy worked at the bank, he put a sign on the door that said, "Gone to dinner, back in 30 minutes." Everyone in town knew that meant he would be back early afternoon. The evening meal was called "supper." We did use the term "lunch" when referring to a lunch box, or the lunch room at school. However, we put our "dinner" in the lunch box and ate "dinner" in the lunch room. If we were going to eat supper out somewhere fancy, my daddy would tell us to "Wear your Sunday go to meeting clothes." That meant "dress up." My grandparents and parents referred to the refrigerator as the "ice box," or the more modern term, "Frigidaire."

There are some words and expressions that I do miss hearing from the past such as "yes sir," and "yes ma'am," as well as several terms of endearment such as "darlin," "honey pie," and "sugar."

When I'm back in the Delta, it takes no more than five minutes for me to slip back into a manner of speech that is as comfortable for me as an old pair of slippers.

Y'all know what I mean, you hear?

**Talk to the Animals:** When I was kid, it was my job to carry food outside to the dogs. When I was four-years-old, I went out to the backyard to feed my daddy's bird dog. I asked Tip if he wanted the red bowl or the green bowl. Tip answered, "The green bowl." I threw the dog bowls into the air, and ran into the house to tell my mother that "Ol' Tip could talk." Even though I tried, I could never again get the bird dog to speak. It was years later that my father confessed that he was in the outhouse and that he had answered for Tip. I wish that he hadn't told me.

## 3 TEEN TIME

**Turning 13:** I was very excited when I officially become a teenager. On the day of my 13th birthday, I walked downtown to Bradsher's Drug Store and bought a Teen magazine and a tube of Clearasil. I had barely reached puberty, and I didn't need the acne medication. I had been led to believe from ads on American Bandstand that all teens needed the product.

Bradsher's Drugstore was a typical small town pharmacy with a soda fountain, assorted sundries, and gift items. Even before turning thirteen, I would sneak an adult magazine from the top of the store's magazine rack, place it inside a Boy's Life Magazine, and look at "dirty" pictures.

I did some of my Christmas shopping at Bradsher's. During the holidays I would go there and purchase "Evening In Paris" perfume as a gift for my schoolteacher. I thought there could be no finer scent.

The drugstore was owned by Don and Beulah Bradsher. Beulah, not liking her given name, went by "Bootie." The couple made a very good living. Each one had a Lincoln Continental car that they kept in a two car garage attached to a blonde brick home. They always had a Great Dane dog as a pet. I remember the sad day when one of their Great Danes, Tillie, was killed on the railroad tracks after being run over by a Cotton Belt Railroad train. Word spread like wildfire about poor Tillie.

I don't know how they got around health regulations, but the Bradshers kept an Amazon parrot named Pappy in the drug store. He sat on top of his cage near the soda fountain. The parrot could talk, but only when he chose to do so. He would threaten to bite off the fingers of children as they stuck them close to him. I too teased Pappy with my finger. He would try to grab it. I would quickly pull it away. It was a game we both enjoyed, and fortunately for me, a game I never lost.

An odd thing about the drugstore was that the far back corner was the liquor section, and the only place in town to buy alcohol. There was a rear entrance to the liquor corner for clients who didn't want to be seen carrying booze out the front door. My parents called it the "Baptist door."

To fulfill another of my teenage obligations, I bought a stereo. I ordered it from the Sears catalogue. It arrived at the post office early one week, and days before my parents could take me to Paragould, a larger town than my hometown of Marmaduke. Paragould had a record store. My town did not. I was desperate to play a record on my new stereo. I needed an album.

I walked downtown to Bradsher's and found the only record in the drug store. It was a Connie Francis album that was attached to a tube of Brylcreem. The record was free if I bought the Brylcreem, an oily crème men's hair ointment that was advertised on the album cover. I purchased it and hurried home to play the record. I played it over and over again. I was amazed at the brilliance of Connie Francis as she sang folk songs.

My parents could not wait for Saturday and our shopping trip to Paragould when I could purchase new records. They had heard Miss Francis sing "Down In The Valley" way too many times. After I purchased several new records, the Connie Francis album disappeared and did not resurface for many years. I did keep the Brylcreem handy and used it proudly until the tube was empty.

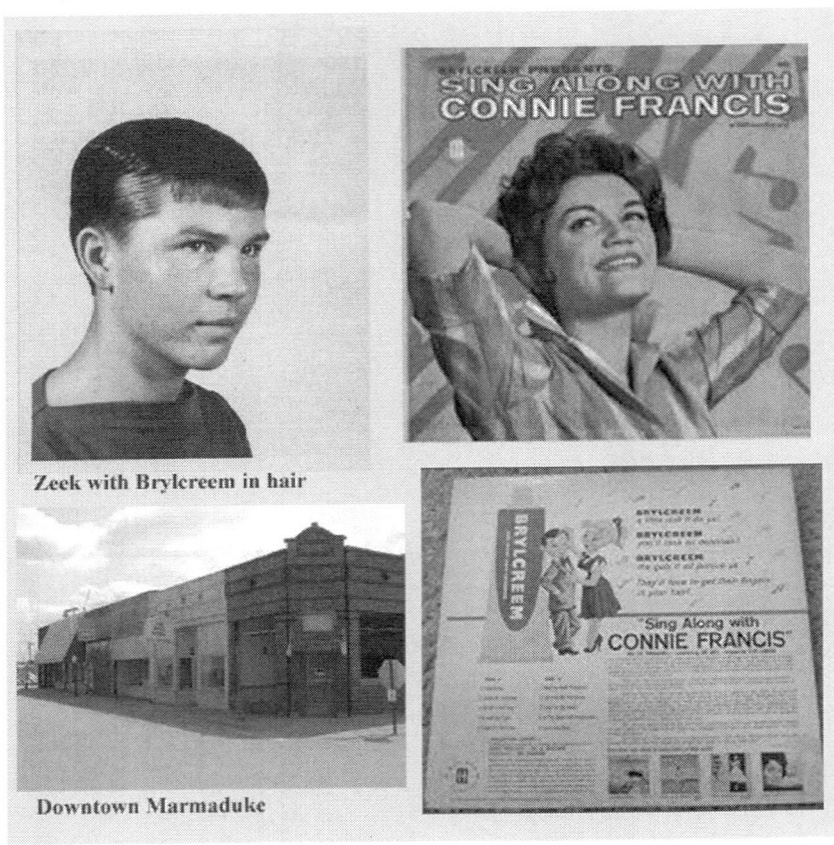

**Zeek with Brylcreem in hair**

**Downtown Marmaduke**

**One Short, One Long:** I was a young teen when telephone service came to my hometown of Marmaduke, Arkansas. Prior to the arrival of phones, news and gossip traveled by word of mouth from neighbor to neighbor.

My mother's beauty shop was attached to our house and because they couldn't call, women would stop by the house to make their hair appointments. The beauty shop was a prime location for hearing and reporting news. The men communicated each morning over coffee at a local café, in the pool hall, or in the barber shop. If there was news of prime importance, word traveled by mouth like wildfire in the small town with a

# Out of the Delta

population of 650 people. Within an hour's time, every citizen had received the news. Before we had phone service, town folk received some of their information by listening to the noon radio show that was broadcast on KDRS from Paragould. Special attention was paid to the obituaries that were read on air.

If there was a fire in town, everyone knew. We heard the siren from our one firetruck, and we would leave our houses and head to the scene of the blaze. Watching burning structures was a community activity.

My daddy was mayor when phone service came to town. Securing the service had been one of his main goals while he was in office. I was very excited about the idea of communicating via the telephone. I had learned from movies and television that talking on the phone was an essential part of being a teenager. When we finally did get our phone, our number was LY7-2221. The LY stood for Lyric.

Unfortunately we were on a party line with an elderly woman, Miss Goforth, who lived down the street. Her ring was two shorts. Ours was one short and one long. I gritted my teeth every time I heard two shorts because I knew the line would be tied up and friends could not call me.

To check if the line was open, I would pick up the receiver, and often I would hear Miss Goforth talking. Usually she was talking about her health. I thought that her conversations were boring. That changed when Miss Goforth, who was in her '80s, found a boyfriend. Then, if I "accidentally" picked up the phone and she was on the line, I found her conversations to be rather interesting. I didn't hear a proposal via the phone line, but when Miss Goforth became engaged, word spread like crazy. The pending nuptials became topic number one in my mother's beauty shop.

Miss Goforth married, sold her home, moved in with her husband, and gave up her phone. I was very happy that she had found love, and I was exceptionally happy for me. I was a teenager, living in a home with a private line. Even though we were no longer on a party line, I still had a problem. I had two teenage sisters who constantly wanted to chat with their friends. Also, my mother wanted to keep the line open so her beauty shop clients could call and make appointments.

Several times a day and for several years, "Get off the Phone," could be heard in the Taylor home. I still got most of my news by word of mouth.

47

**Dents and Bruises:** When I turned fourteen, I wanted wheels. I was two years away from getting my driver's license at the age of sixteen, the legal age to drive a car. However, in the state of Arkansas, a person could operate certain small motorized vehicles without a license. Included in the category were mopeds and very small motorbikes.

I turned to my "go to" source, the Sears catalogue, and I found a small Allstate motorbike that fit the bill. The bike was bright red, small, and was perfect for a scrawny fourteen-year-old. The price was $125. I used money that I had saved from picking cotton and ordered the bike.

The bike arrived in two large cardboard boxes. I was surprised that it arrived in two pieces. After unpacking it, my father helped me put the pieces together. I took a quick glance at the manual and read how to mix the proper proportion of oil and gasoline. I put the mixture in the tank. I was so anxious to take the bike for a spin, I didn't bother to read the rest of the manual and learn the proper operating procedures.

I kick started the bike, and I took off at a jaunty pace. The controls were rather touchy, and I accelerated at a breakneck speed. A half block into my journey, I tried to locate the brake. Before I could stop the bike, I ran into a ditch and was thrown over the handle bars. I escaped serious injury. However, I did have a bruise that ran from my knee up to my waist.

I was proud of my injury. I described the wreck to my friends as "my near brush with death." My little bike suffered a dented fender. That hurt worse than my bruised leg. The night of my wreck, I read the rest of the operating manual.

**Tan my Hide:** In the '60s it was not only fashionable to have a tan, it was thought to be good for one's health. Beach movies starring Annette Funicello and Frankie Avalon along with the surfing themed music of the Beach Boys, convinced me and my friends that in order to be "with it," we should be bronze colored.

It didn't matter that we lived in the Arkansas Delta and very far from any ocean.

In the summer my friends and I would lie in the sun on quilts in our

Above: Ingredients for tanning lotion

Right: getting ready to remove shirt and bask.

## Out of the Delta

backyards. We slathered our bodies with a concoction of baby oil and staining iodine. We did not wear sunscreen. That would have slowed down the tanning process. We applied lemon juice to our hair thinking it would speed up the sun's bleaching of our locks.

School was not in session during September and October so students could pick cotton at harvest time. Therefore, we were in school in July and August. School during the summer months let out at one p.m. That left plenty of time in the afternoon to devote to tanning.

Although the temperature was very hot and the humidity was stifling during summer in the Delta, nothing would stop us from achieving our quest for a Hollywood tan. A nearby hose connected to an outdoor faucet was available for an occasional misting. When the temps became unbearable, I would run an extension cord from the kitchen and hook up an electric fan.

Proper sunbathing also required listening to a transistor radio. In the Delta the radio was always tuned to our favorite Memphis AM rock station WHBQ, a station famous for airing Elvis's first record "That's Alright Mama."

My best tan did not come from the sun. While at school I noticed dark stains on the arms and hands of some of the students. The dark stains were caused by rubbing walnut husks on the skin in order to kill ringworm. Using walnut husk juice was a folk cure. I don't know whether or not the cure was effective. However, I did know that it made the skin a beautiful brown color.

My friend Donnie lived on the North edge of town. There was a huge walnut tree behind his family's barn. I told him that I knew a way to get a quick, dark, tan by using the walnut husks. He agreed to give my plan a try.

Late that summer we went behind his barn and found a bumper crop of walnuts on the ground. There were no nearby neighbors so we stripped down, husked some walnuts, and began "staining" each other. We wore gloves so that we wouldn't overly stain our hands. Although the husks were somewhat abrasive, and it took a while to evenly cover each other's bodies, the final result would have made Frankie Avalon jealous.

We made plans to attend a late afternoon softball game that evening. To create the best contrast with our bronzed skin, we wore white shorts and white tank style tee-shirts. We arrived at the ball field shortly before dusk, knowing that the soft light of sunset was the best time to show off a tan. Everyone at the game raved about our tanned bodies. We never gave away our bronzing secret.

I had never surfed and had never seen the ocean, but that summer evening I felt totally like a beach bum with my walnut toned skin.

We can go anywhere our minds take us. Surfs up.

**Bejeweled:** I went to High School in the little Delta town of Marmaduke, Arkansas. Across the street was a small café named "Nettie's." It was considered an "honor" to work at Nettie's, and I was lucky enough to work there during lunch and after school. I received fifty cents an hour and free food.

The little diner complete with a juke box served sandwiches. A hot dog cost a dime, a chili dog was 15 cents, a hamburger cost twenty cents, and a bar-b-cue sandwich was a quarter. The owner, Nettie Lambert, cooked a roast each morning that she used for making the bar-b-cue. We also sold cokes, milk, candy, chips, and some school supplies. We sold cigarettes for two cents each. A pack of cigarettes was 25 cents. Nettie made an extra 15 cents per package by selling them for two cents each. It was illegal to break the package seal, but we did it anyway.

Left: Marmaduke High School
Below: My sister with pierced ears

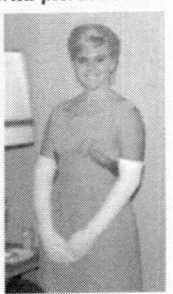

Nettie always wore long dangly earrings in her pierced ears at a time when only carnival workers and gypsies had pierced ears. When she was young, she had pierced her ears with an ice pick. Inspired by Nettie's dangly earrings, my sister decided that she too wanted pierced ears.

I volunteered to do the piercing. I numbed her ear with an ice cube, put a bar of soap behind her lobe, and pushed a sewing needle complete with thread through her ear lobe. It did hurt, but she was brave enough to let me do the other one. Immediately after the piercing, I removed the thread and placed a gold earring in each ear. We used lots of rubbing alcohol to prevent infection.

The next day at school, my sister received lots of attention and I received lots of requests from her friends for me to pierce their ears. Over the course of a few weeks, I pierced the ears of 40 or more of our friends. I did the "operations" at night in my mother's beauty shop. I'm proud to say, inspired by Nettie, that I helped bejewel Marmaduke High.

**Racing in Slow Time:** When I was a child, I couldn't wait for my mother to finish work on Saturday afternoons. When she got through, my family would get in the family car, and my father would drive us the ten miles to the nearest Kroger's in Paragould, Arkansas. That's where my mother, coupons in hand, would do her weekly grocery shopping. With each purchase she collected Top Value stamps that she carefully licked and glued into books to later redeem for merchandise. While she shopped, my younger sister and I made a quick trip to Ben Franklin's to buy a ten-cent toy, stop at a little food stand for a foot long hot dog, x-ray our feet at the Red Goose shoe store, and rejoin my father who never left the car. I knew he was nipping on the Old Crow whiskey that he kept hidden under his seat. I could smell it on his breath when I got back into the car.

I enjoyed sitting in the car with my daddy because I thought he was the smartest man in the world. I believed that he knew just about everything because he could identify each automobile that passed by us on Pruett Street. He would say, "Here comes a Chevy," or "That's a Ford." Every now and then I would blurt out, "That one's a Pontiac." It was the only car I could identify because of the car's distinctive hood ornament that depicted a stylized head of the Indian Chief Pontiac.

My daddy was not brand loyal when it came to purchasing cars. However, he was "color loyal" and bought autos in his favorite color of pink. When I was in grade school, our family car was a 52 Ford sedan that was pink with a cream colored top and a fancy Hollywood tire on the rear bumper. The next car that my father bought was a pink 1957 Chevy station wagon that once again had a cream colored top. By the time I was ready to drive, my father had purchased a coral pink 1959 Chevrolet Impala with a cream top.

There was not a driver's education course where I went to school. My father taught me to drive on a two lane country road. The Impala did have an automatic transmission. That made it easier to drive especially on the hilly roads of Crowley's Ridge that bordered the west side of town. However, the car was as long as a "whore's dream" (one of my father's favorite expressions.) The length of the car made it difficult for me to parallel park.

The week that I turned 16, I took my driver's test. I had spent many hours studying the driver's manual to prepare for the written test. I was excited the morning of the test. I was also very nervous. The state trooper who administered the test was a large man who somewhat intimidated me by his size and authoritarian demeanor. I received a perfect score on the written test and aced the driving test with one exception: parallel parking. I knocked over both flags that denoted the parking space. The trooper said, "Close enough. You are trying to park a very long car." I was no longer intimidated by the man and thought, "Gosh, he is really sweet."

In anticipation of receiving my license, I had managed to save $300 of my cotton picking money to buy a car. Unlike my father, I didn't pick out a pink one. I bought a baby blue, six cylinder, automatic, 1952 Ford.

While many of my friends drove eight cylinder hot rods, I was very content cruising around in my little Ford. For a six cylinder, it was fairly peppy. Guys from my school often went down the highway to the mile crossing to drag race. The mile crossing was the first place on the highway where the road crossed over the Cotton Belt Railroad tracks. If someone said, "Meet me at the mile crossing," I knew they were going to race. I didn't stand a chance racing my car against hot rods. However, I knew that I did stand a chance of winning at George Ray's Drag Strip in Paragould.

George Ray's was a legal racing venue that was heavily attended Sunday afternoons by folks from several surrounding Delta counties. Admission was charged for attending, and some illegal betting took place. The race track was paved and was a quarter mile long. Two cars raced at a time when given the "start signal" by George Ray who served as the flagman.

At the track, there were several classifications for the competing cars depending on horsepower, and whether they had been altered or were stock. Letters denoted the classification with AA being for the fastest and most powerful. AA/Stock was for the highest factory rated horsepower cars. My little Ford was in the slowest stock category. It was classified as N/Stock Automatic. Despite that classification, my car was the fastest in its class and I never lost a race.

I was proud of the trophies that I won. They were wooden, had a George Ray's Drag metal logo on them, and had a metal automobile on the top of each one. I displayed them in my bedroom. I couldn't have been more proud of the trophies if I had won them while driving a Corvette.

Despite limitations, there are times that we can use "what we got" and we still can come out as a "winner."

In 2006, George Ray's Drag Strip was listed on the National Register of Historic Places. George Ray passed away in 2009.

**I Could Dance Like Nobody Else:** My parents loved to dance. Once a month on a Saturday night, they dressed up, and drove to the Kingsway Supper Club in Paragould, Arkansas, where they danced the night away. I thought that my mother looked like a movie star when she donned her fancy dance clothes.

My sisters and I inherited my parents' love of dance. My mother taught me the dances that she knew including the Charleston. Other ballroom dances were learned when my sisters and I attended weekly classes at the Westbrook School of Dance in Paragould. We learned the waltz, bop, cha cha, rumba, samba and more. To keep up with the latest dance fads, I watched the American Bandstand television show. I was the first in town to do the twist. I had twist shoes with rotating discs on the soles.

There was little opportunity to dance in the little town where I lived. Dancing was not allowed at school. Saturday evenings, my friends and I would turn my mother's beauty shop into a dance hall. The only other place in town to dance was at the Methodist Church Fellowship Hall at dances sponsored by the Methodist Youth Fellowship. I came from a long line of Methodists so I felt right at home at the dance parties while my Baptist friends who attended, seemed to be a little nervous. We kept their attendance secret from their parents.

One of the best days of my teen life was when I got my driver's license, and I could drive to nearby towns to attend teenage dances. On the very first Saturday after turning sixteen, friends piled into my newly purchased car. We went to Jonesboro, Arkansas, where we attended our first real teen dance with music performed by a live band.

**Above: My mother dressed to go dancing**

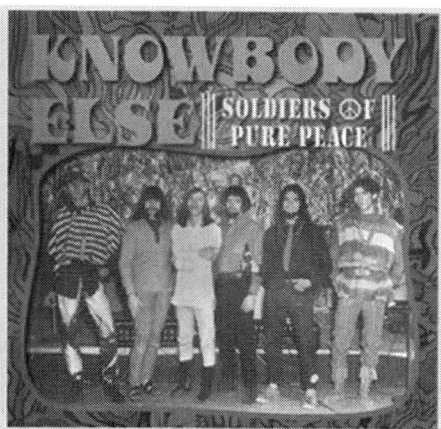

**Above: Knowbody Else, later known as Black Oak Arkansas**

One of our favorite places to dance was in an enclosed pavilion at Reynolds Park in Paragould, Arkansas. It was there where I met James Mangrum and his friends who lived in nearby Black Oak, Arkansas. They were in the process of forming a band that became the "Knowbody Else." They quickly became my favorite band, and I became a groupie. If they were playing anywhere within driving distance, I would be at their gig.

Their fan base grew as did their fame. The band signed a record deal with Stax records in 1969 and moved to Memphis. In 1970, they moved to Los Angeles, signed a contract with ATCO records, and changed the band's name to "Black Oak Arkansas." In 1971 they released an album by the same name, "Black Oak Arkansas." James Mangrum became known as Jim Dandy. In the 1970s, the band released ten albums that "charted." BOA became known as one of the leading southern rock bands, and a pioneer in that genre. The group earned three gold records. In 1975 I saw Black Oak Arkansas in concert in the Mid-South Coliseum in Memphis. They played to a sold out crowd of 10,000.

I stood up in the aisle and danced.

**Tender Hearted Chicken Farmer:** During my freshman year in high school, I took a year of agriculture class. I wasn't interested in farming, but I needed to take the course to get enough credits to graduate. The little school that I attended did not have art, music, or language courses and in the 1960s, boys did not take home economics. I had no other option but to study agriculture.

While in Ag class, I watched films that taught activities that I knew I would never practice, including a film that graphically explained how to castrate a hog. I did learn one thing during agriculture class that came in handy later. I learned to weld. I used that knowledge while in sculpture class in art school. Every boy in my Ag class had to have a year-long project.

Most of the students chose to raise an acre of cotton. I lived in town, and I didn't have an acre of cotton. I decided I would raise chickens. My daddy and I put up a fence and built a chicken house in our backyard. When it was completed, I went to the local feed store and bought twenty baby Rhode Island Red chicks. The clerk placed the little fowl into a cardboard box. While walking the three blocks back home, I petted the chicks to comfort them. I was thinking, "These babies are adorable."

I kept a record book about my project, recorded the cost of chicken food, hours of labor spent, and other expenses incurred. At the end of the school year, I was to kill the chickens, dress them, and weigh them. Following that gruesome task, I was to go to the grocery store, check the price per pound of dressed chicken, multiply the price by the pounds of my dressed birds, deduct my expenses, and determine if I made a profit.

There was no way that I was going to kill my chickens. Many of them had names and all were pets. The lady who had been my first grade teacher, Miss Versa Butler, had a "fun farm" out in the country, and she came to my rescue. She let me move my chickens to her place. They lived out the rest of their lives on her farm. I had visitation rights.

After the relocation, I had no choice but to lie to my Ag teacher. I turned in my record book showing that I made a slight profit. I received a passing grade. I knew then that chicken farming was not going to be my calling. I chose instead to go into the arts, a profession where I can honestly declare, "No animals were harmed during the creation of this painting."

Right: Chicken Painting

Below right: Rhode Island Reds.

Above: Agriculture class. I'm sitting at front table, wearing white socks.

**This Fragile Life:** While I was a young man, death came a-calling. I was sitting in history class in high school one spring morning when the principle came in and asked to speak to one of my classmates.

Soon we heard screaming. The weather was warm and all the windows were open. Everyone in class rushed to the open windows when we heard my classmate, Willie Mae, and her sister screaming and crying while being led away from campus. Their father had accidentally run over their four-year-old sister, Jackie, with a plow after she had fallen from a tractor while riding behind him.

Our class had only thirty-three members, and we were a very close knit group. We didn't know how to react to the tragedy. Some of us just sat and cried. Many of us had lost elderly family members, but we were not prepared to lose someone in our community who was young.

A few short years later while I was a freshman in college, death came calling once again and took another young person. I was just beginning my life's journey as a young adult, when one of my dear friends ended her journey. Sonya, a beautiful, sweet woman who I had once dated, passed away as a result of a terrible accident.

One Saturday night she received an engagement ring from a young man. The next morning on their way to church, engagement ring on her finger, the couple was involved in a head-on collision.

Sonya's fiancée had suffered minor injuries. She had suffered severe head injuries. Due to the severity of her injuries, she was transported to a hospital in Memphis and placed on life support. Sonya did not survive.

Friends of Sonya: Brenda, Jim Bob, Rhonda (my sister,) and Sonya on the ground.

Sonya

Her body was sent to the local funeral home. Her family decided to have her laid out in an open casket so that her friends could see her one more time. Her head had been shaved while in the hospital. The funeral home had put a wig on her. When I viewed her body, all I could see in my mind's eye was how she once had looked.

The custom at the time was that the deceased was not to be left unattended. The night before the funeral, a few friends and I sat up all night with Sonya's body. During the wake, we cried, we laughed, we loved, and we realized how fleeting life was for all of us. I realized that I was no longer immortal. Every day counts.

**Taking it off for the 4th of July:** For many years, Marmaduke, Arkansas has celebrated the 4th of July with an annual picnic. The celebration features bands, political speeches, bar-b-cue, and beauty contests. The picnic was established as a benefit event to raise money for the upkeep of the area's cemeteries. Proper maintenance of the final resting places of loved ones is very important to the folks in the Delta.

During the sixties, one method of raising money for the picnic and for the cemeteries was to sell "chances" to win a new car that had been donated by a local dealership. The winning "chance" would be drawn as the finale of the picnic. I spent part of one summer driving the car here and there in the Delta. My sister, one of our friends, and I would take the car to nearby towns and go door-to-door and business to business, selling the chances. The law considered selling chances to be an illegal gambling activity, so we asked for "donations." For each "donation" of one dollar, the donor received a free chance to win the car. For each book of 40 chances that we sold, we earned four dollars for ourselves.

The annual picnic was a much anticipated event, and when I was a kid, the holiday was one of my favorite days of the year. Even after graduating from high school and moving away, when possible I returned to Marmaduke on the 4th of July. In 1966 while home from college, I was asked to be the escort to the reigning Miss Arkansas. She was making a guest appearance, and because my father was chair of the picnic committee that year, I was chosen to be her escort. It's always "who you know."

The best years at the picnic were the ones when the town was able to secure a carnival that would set up a few days prior to the 4th. When I was 16-years-old, a carnival was at the picnic. Along with the usual rides, games, and side shows, there was also a girlie show. Many of the townsfolk were outraged. I was excited and chomping at the bit to go to the show.

Above: Mid-South Fair     Above: Fairgrounds in Marmaduke, site of 4th of July Picnic

The Mid-South Fair was held each fall in Memphis. I attended several times. My favorite part of the fair was the side shows. I was particularly intrigued by the girlie shows. Often the beautiful burlesque dancers were paraded in front of their tents for a teaser preview. One year the barker had two pitches. He said, "This beautiful girl does the splits over a watermelon and it completely disappears." Turning to another dancer, he said, "And this lovely girl wears a costume that is made from fabric that costs fifty dollars a yard. However, she only wears fifty cents worth." Oh how I wanted to see that, but alas, I was too young to buy a ticket. Even though I was only 16 the year that the girlie show came to the Marmaduke picnic, I thought, "This is my best chance to see some strippers."

The picnic ended at 10 p.m. with the drawing for the car, and a fireworks display. The carnival was still open, but most folks went home. I walked the few blocks to my house with my parents, told them I was tired, and went to my bedroom. After I knew everyone in the household was asleep, I got out of bed and dressed. My bedroom was at the rear of the house. A couple of years earlier, I secretly had moved the hinges on one of the window screens so that it opened like a screen door. I would often crawl out through my window, and I would go for late night strolls,

That night, around 11:30, I went out through the window and walked back to the carnival. The girlie show had advertised a "Midnight Rambling Show," that would be the best show of the day. I paid my two dollars, lied about my age, walked in and took my seat. I certainly didn't look like I was 18, the age for admittance. Even though I was 16, I looked about 14. The ticket seller didn't care. He just wanted my money.

There were quite a few men in the audience. I knew several of them, but I trusted that they wouldn't snitch on me for being there. To do so would have also incriminated them. The dancers were all African American ladies. Three were svelte lovely women who skillfully danced while they moved scarves and feathers so that nothing illegal and forbidden was revealed. I was amazed and appreciative of their talents. They each danced a couple of times before the star dancer came on stage to do her number.

Her name was Shirley. She weighed about three-hundred pounds and was billed as "Shirley in the Temple, a performer who can jiggle things that other dancers don't have." And she did. I was mesmerized by her skillful performance. I left the tent happy that my curiosity about burlesque had finally been satisfied.

I learned three things: Anticipating the forbidden is often more exciting than experiencing the real thing: where there's a will, there's a way: and from Shirley, "Use what you got."

**First Real Job:** I graduated from high school at the age of seventeen. I was a scrawny 115 pounds, a small guy with big plans that included college in the fall. Prior to graduating, I had picked cotton each fall while in school. That year, I would be in college during the harvest season, and for the first time, I needed a "real job" to help pay school expenses. When I say "real job," I mean one where I would work by the clock and not by the sun like I had done while working in the field.

My Daddy had a friend who was a foreman in an aircraft plant located in a nearby town. Through that connection, Daddy got me a summer job at the factory. I started at $1.47 an hour and when I got my paycheck, I was very disappointed when after taxes, I had only cleared $47 per week. I made much more than that while picking cotton, a job where no taxes were withheld, and everyone was paid in cash.

I hated my job. Work in the plant started at 7 a.m. Each worker had to be standing by their appointed machines at 6:55 a.m. so that when the whistle sounded, there was not one second of work missed. The plant was not air conditioned and it was extremely hot during that summer in the Arkansas Delta. Hot as it was, I had to wear long sleeve shirts to keep my arms from being burned by flying sparks. I operated a machine that drilled a long narrow groove into an aluminum frame that was part of a helicopter motor mount. I guided the drill with one hand while squirting kerosene on the drill to keep it from balling up. The fumes were horrific. It took about five minutes to do each one, followed quickly by the next one.

I went to work day after day, and I detested every minute of it. Not wanting to be a quitter and not wanting to disappoint my father, I kept the job for the entire summer. I learned two things from working there: I was determined to stay in college and never have to work in a factory ever again, and from then on, I would find my own job.

**Dark and Exotic:** Following active duty in World War II, my mother's two brothers returned to Arkansas and a bleak economy. They could not find employment. Like many young men from the region, they moved to Michigan and worked in the automobile plants. They each married women from Michigan, had children, and made a life up north. Each summer, they returned to Arkansas for yearly visits with their southern family.

One of my mother's brothers, Uncle Lowell, married an Arab-American woman. Her name was Betty. She was a wonderful woman and a beloved member of our extended family. My Aunt Betty and Uncle Lowell lived in the Detroit suburb of Warren. The Arab-American neighborhood where they lived extended for blocks and blocks.

Uncle Lowell and Aunt Betty had three children. Their oldest son, Jimmy, was near my age, and we became close friends. My female classmates looked forward to his yearly summer visits. My friends, like me, were very waspish. Jimmy had black hair and a dark complexion. He was very exotic looking. The Arkie girls compared him to Frankie Avalon and Sal Mineo, and they vied for his attention. Sometimes, it is good to be different. Also, it is good for me to come clean and confess: "I have half-Yankee cousins." There, I feel better.

Above: Family reunion, Paragould, AR, I'm second from left and Jimmy is far right.

Above: Cousin Jimmy

**Hair Everywhere:** I grew up with a beauty shop attached to my boyhood home in Northeast Arkansas. My mother's shop was one door away from our living room. Her customers would often stroll through our living room on the way to the family bathroom. The women would interrupt our TV viewing with their small talk, and they tracked hair onto the living room floor. Hair seemed to be everywhere. As a kid, I played on the linoleum floor in the beauty shop rolling my toy cars through the hair clippings. We would burn the swept up hair along with other combustibles in a burn barrel in the backyard. The hair would sizzle and pop while burning, and it released a horrid stench.

However, I liked having the beauty shop attached to the family home. It gave me ample opportunity to play with hair color, not only on myself but on the hair of my friends. When my sister was in the seventh grade, I bleached her hair to a platinum shade. She kept it that color for many years. My sister's boyfriend was kicked off the basketball team after I bleached his hair. It was permissible for girls to be blond but not basketball players.

Another one of my friends was sent home from school after I colored his hair cardinal red. I had to quickly fix it before he was allowed to go back to class.

I had friends who were identical twins. They lived in the nearby town of Rector. They were very good looking blond headed boys, and they were next to impossible to tell apart. I thought I was doing them a favor after dying one of the boy's hair jet black so that he would be different from his brother. Their mother didn't agree. The morning after the dye job, she woke the boys for school, saw the black haired twin, and scared her entire neighborhood with her screams.

Hairstyles that I've worn through the years. All were cut by my mother.

My father went to Irby's Barber Shop to have his hair cut. He said it was only fair since the barber's wife, Cricket, had my mother do her weekly shampoo and set. I think my father actually went to the barber shop for the gossip and because it was "the manly thing to do." I didn't go to the barber shop. My mother cut my hair. The first time I had someone else cut my hair was when I visited relatives in Amarillo. My uncle was in the air force, and I had my hair cut on base. I was scalped and vowed to never again let anyone but my mother touch my hair.

Unfortunately, I forgot that vow the next summer when an Eskimo boy from Alaska came to Arkansas to visit friends. He told me he knew how to cut hair. He asked if I wanted him to trim mine. I said, "Sure." I was very trusting and I was thinking, "How often does one have the chance to get their hair cut by an Eskimo?" He took the electric clippers to my head, cut a swath down the center, laughed, and said he was only kidding. I had to have the rest of my hair buzzed off to even it up.

After the two bad haircut experiences, I learned my lesson and would only allow my mother to cut my hair. I knew that my mother would do exactly what I wanted to have done, no more and no less. When I grew my hair halfway down my back, she would, as requested, barely trim the ends.

While I was enrolled as a student in the Memphis College of Art, I had a friend who went to New York City on vacation and returned to school sporting a shag haircut. The heavily layered look was the latest hairstyle of the day. I wanted one. I found a photo of pop star David Cassidy who sported the cut. I drove to my mother's house in Marmaduke the next weekend, showed her the picture of Cassidy, and had her cut my hair to look like his. It was perfect. I was definitely "styling my shag."

I could always trust my mother to trim my hair just right, and she did up until the day that she died at the age of 88.

Trust is everything.

**Empty Nest Except for a Chocolate Poodle**: My two sisters and I moved from my parents' home during an eight month period in 1964. My older sister married and moved into a farmhouse with her new husband. As planned, I started college that September and moved into a dorm at Arkansas State University. What was not planned was that my 16-year-old sister would also move out of the house that year.

My sister Rhonda never liked school, and she seemed restless living in our small town. When she received a proposal from a young man who she had dated for only a short while, she said, "Yes." The suitor had graduated from high school with my class and had moved to West Hollywood to work for his grandfather. I suspected that my sister saw marriage as a way to quit school, and to move to California. However, she said, "I want to marry him because I love him."

My parents threw a fit and refused to give their consent. I was upset as well and I told her, "This is crazy and don't expect me to go to the wedding." The family was in turmoil. My daddy sought guidance from his father who was a Methodist minister. My wise grandfather told my parents, "If you don't give her your consent, she will likely run away to California, and you might not see her again." After much thought, my parents accepted his advice and gave the marriage their blessing. After my parents change of heart, I softened and told my relieved sister, "I will go to your wedding."

My sister and I had always been very close, and I only wanted her to be happy. She planned a Christmas day ceremony, a time when her finance would be back in Arkansas visiting his parents. I thought, "Damn, now she's going to ruin Christmas." I gave the marriage six months.

The day after the wedding, the newlyweds headed for California. I was home for holiday break until after the New Year. That New Year's Eve, I stayed home with my mother. I knew that my father would be in bed long before midnight, and I didn't want Mama to be sitting alone when the New Year came in. On the big console TV in the living room, we watched the ball drop in Times Square. The next day we ate black-eyed peas and cabbage with hopes of a prosperous New Year. My mother was wishing she had her baby girl back home.

Below, my sister and my brother-in-law on their wedding day.

Six months later she got her wish. Things went bust in California, and the newlyweds returned to Arkansas. They arrived in my parents' driveway in a Buick that died on the spot. They had paid $95 for the car. My sister was holding a toy chocolate poodle that they had purchased while passing through Oklahoma. They had paid $100 for the puppy, and that expenditure had left them with five dollars to their name.

For a while they lived in a trailer near my parents. After my brother-in-law got a job driving a milk truck, they moved to a nearby town. Their landlord didn't allow pets. They couldn't take the poodle with them. They left him with my mother. She loved the dog and because of his presence, her house was no longer empty of a "child." She had a fur baby, a poodle named Cho Cho.

When my sister passed away in 2013, she had been married to the same man for 49 years. Together they had three children, and six grandchildren.

I had given their marriage six-months. I learned that I wasn't so smart, I could not predict the future, and I didn't know what was in another's heart. True love has lasting power.

**Fearful Peacenik Afraid to Come Out:** I knew from an early age that I was gay. When I was a teen, I felt compelled to keep my orientation a secret. I wasn't ready for rejection, ridicule, and the probable bullying that would have awaited me. I would rather have died than to come out. I lived a lie. I lived in fear of exposure.

When I turned 18 years of age, it was mandatory for all males to take their military physical. It was during the Vietnam War years, and the draft was in place. I was in my first year of college when I had to return to my hometown, board a bus with other 18-year-old males with whom I had grown up, and go to Memphis for the military physical.

Facing the physical, I was very distraught. I had always considered myself to be a pacifist. Being in the military would have been foreign to my nature. My dream had been to serve in the Peace Corp. I really wanted to make a difference. However, that dream was not possible for me. Being in the Peace Corp was one way to get a deferment from the military. Only rich boys with pull could join the Corp. I was far from rich.

I had been told that if I ate lots of sugar, I would flunk the physical because my sugar level would show me to be diabetic. I ate a five pound bag of sugar the night before the physical. The next morning I boarded a yellow school bus for the journey to the old Veterans Administration Hospital on Getwell Avenue in Memphis. After arriving, I saw hundreds of young men who were also there for physicals. I studied their faces and I could sense that I was not the only one who was nervous. The physical took most of the day and was humiliating. We were herded naked from room to room and examined by numerous doctors.

I did have an option that would allow me to flunk the physical. I could check the "box." By checking the "box," one admitted that they were homosexual, and they would receive a 4F status: unfit for service. I had been told that guys who checked the box would be kept overnight for psychiatric evaluation. At the time homosexuality was considered a mental disorder. I thought that the guys from home would know that I was gay if I checked the box. They would have noticed I wasn't on the bus for the return trip. The sugar trick did not work. I passed the physical.

As long as I stayed in school, I had a student deferment. After graduation, I was able to obtain an occupational deferment because I was able to secure a teaching job. That's not what I had planned to do as a profession, but I gladly took the job in order to avoid the draft.

In 1969, the government decided that they would conduct a lottery to decide who would be drafted. On December 1st, 1969, I sat with many young men in a student lounge on the campus of Washington University in Saint Louis where I was attending night classes. We watched on TV as the lottery took place. During the broadcast, a military person drew from a container a birth date that was enclosed in a blue capsule. Each drawn birth date was then matched to a number that determined who would be drafted. That year, all birthdays that matched a number below 195, were eligible. Young men who received the lowest numbers were taken immediately. There were cheers and groans as the numbers were drawn. I won the lottery. My number was 281.

After watching the lottery I left the lounge, and I went home alone to my apartment. My future once again belonged to me. I was elated. However, I cried while thinking about the young men who were not as fortunate as I had been during the drawing. Lying in my bed with eyes closed, I could still see the despair on their faces. I saw fear.

No longer subject to the draft, I was able to quit teaching and to return to school. I enrolled in the Memphis College of Art as a painting major. I was able to resume my goal to become a fine artist. I vowed to myself to never again "deny who I am," even in the face of death.

In reality, "That ain't living."

# 4 FAMILY

**Long Journey Home:** My great-grandfather, Julius Alonzo Ogles, was born in Benton County, Tennessee, in 1871. In 1900 he left Tennessee in a covered wagon with my great-grandmother, Vashti, and their four children. The family crossed the Mississippi River on a ferry. They were traveling to Indian Territory where they planned to claim available land and build a new life in the Great West. Indian Territory bordered the western boundary of Arkansas. The area became Oklahoma in 1907.

When they arrived at the territory, my great-grandfather was disappointed in the quality of the soil. The dirt where they had lived in Tennessee had been rich and black. Their oldest child, my grandmother, told me that the family was afraid of the Indians, and that wolves would follow their wagon at night. They turned around, crossed the Arkansas border, and headed back toward Tennessee. During the return trip, my great-grandfather noticed that the soil in Northeast Arkansas was rich and black. Not wanting to cross the Mississippi river again, he decided they would settle there. He never left.

By the time I was born, Julius Alonzo Ogles was an elderly widower who lived on the edge of town with his daughter, my grandmother, Eva Belle Harvey. His many grandchildren and great-grandchildren called him "Grandpa." My grandmother was called "Mom."

Grandpa and Mom had electricity in their little house, but there was no indoor plumbing. The only heat source was a potbellied stove in the living room. Grandpa would get up at 4 a.m. and start a fire in the potbellied stove during the winter months. Early mornings all year long he would start a fire in the wood burning kitchen stove so it would be good and hot, and ready for Mom to bake biscuits for breakfast.

I enjoyed spending the night with them. I thought it was fun taking a bath in a galvanized tub in the kitchen in water that had been heated on the cook stove. When my younger sister and I stayed with them, an evening treat was popcorn popped atop the wood stove. My sister, Mom, and I would play cards. Even though we were not gambling and only playing "Old Maid" or "Authors," my great-grandfather would not play with us. He thought playing cards might border on being sinful and he wasn't going to take a chance. There was no television in their house, and only one radio. While the three of us played cards, Grandpa sat in his rocker and listened to gospel shows on an old AM radio. Even though the programs were in English, the shows were broadcast from Mexico.

When I was eight-years-old, Grandpa and Mom moved to a house inside the city limits. For the first time in their lives, they were living in a house with indoor plumbing. During warm months, he spent most afternoons sitting on the front porch in a rocker, smoking his pipe, and watching the world go by. When he would go into the house, he would leave his lit pipe on the porch. My cousins and I would then take turns sneaking puffs from the pipe.

I was thirteen when my great-grandfather passed away. He died in the house following several days of being bed-ridden. The doctor dropped by each day to check on him. The doctor reported, "Nothing can be done, it's just a matter of time." On his last day to live, a low almost growling sound came from his throat. The old timers said it was the "death rattle" and that he would soon be gone. He died early that evening.

After he passed away, my grandmother had him laid out in the front bedroom of her house. The wake went on for three days. The family had removed the bed to make room for the casket, and the mirrors in the room were covered in black cloth. There were people there 24 hours a day to sit with the body. The undertakers, a husband and wife team, would come to the house once a day with a make-up kit to freshen the body.

After having his body laid out in that room, his great-grand-kids refused to ever sleep in there again. We loved our great-grandpa, but we were still afraid of his ghost.

Above: My Great-Grandfather, Julius Alonzo Ogles, "Grandpa"

Above right: Grandpa, my Great-Grandmother, Vashti, and my grandmother "Mom," Eva Belle Harvey

Bottom right: Last home

**Dress Pants:** My fraternal grandfather Garland Cicero Taylor was a Methodist preacher, fairly liberal, fun, and jolly. He was born in Lawrence County, Arkansas in 1886. He had attended school in a log cabin, and he went to a church that dated back to 1815. He related that when he was young, "Men sat on one side of the church and women on the other. Nary an ankle could be seen." The church was served by circuit riders. The circuit riders were preachers who served several churches. They traveled on horseback. My grandfather was influenced by the traveling preachers, and he got "the calling." He gave up six-hundred acres, his mules, and went into the ministry.

During my grandfather's career, he was assigned to several different parishes in eastern Arkansas. They were always within a couple of hours driving distance from my family's home. We would visit my grandparents every couple of months on a Sunday, and we would arrive at their home, a parsonage, in time to attend church. The only time that my father went to church is when we visited his parents or they visited us. He said, "I had enough of that while growing up."

My grandmother in her role as a pastor's wife was more reserved. We referred to her as "Grandmother Taylor." She came from a Dutch family and she stuck to what was deemed proper. I was not allowed to wear blue jeans to my Grandmother Taylor's house. She thought that jeans were not proper attire for a young man to wear on the "Lord's day." While I hated wearing dress pants, my mother made me wear them when we went to see my grandparents. I was instructed to not get the trousers torn or stained, a difficult task for an active boy. I was to sit quietly and to not go in and out of the house too often for fear of letting in a fly.

When my grandfather retired, my grandparents moved to Osceola, Arkansas. He did continue to preach as a guest pastor well into his 90s. His mind remained sharp. He once said, "While most old folk have trouble with their minds, my problem is on the other end. My feet hurt."

I can't remember when Rosie, a beautiful African American woman, joined the family as my grandparent's maid. My youngest sister Rhonda and I were very energetic children. We found it very difficult to sit still and be proper during our visits to our grandparents' home. We often sought refuge in the kitchen where Rosie spent most of her time. Rosie pampered us, and loved us. We loved her in return.

Soon after my grandmother's death, my Grandfather Taylor, at the age of 76, announced that he would remarry. I crossed my fingers and hoped it would be to Rosie. Unfortunately, it was not. Drat.

**Michigan Relatives:** My great-aunt Precious Beulah didn't like her name. She preferred for us to call her "Boober." She was my grandmother's sister and the youngest of her siblings. After World War II, Boober, along with her brother, two of my mother's brothers, and one of my mother's cousins, left the Arkansas Delta for Detroit. The men all moved to Michigan to work in the automobile plants. There were no jobs at that time in their home state. The women in the family were expected to stay home in Arkansas. Boober was rebellious by nature and insisted on moving north with the men. She was what my father called, "A rounder."

Northern life suited her, and it let her be herself: a woman who smoked cigarettes, drank, and played honky-tonk piano. She even married twice, the first woman in the family to do so. She owned several poodles and, she always had a parakeet or two. She crocheted like a fiend. She made us laugh and we loved her to pieces. She remained in Michigan until her death in 1979.

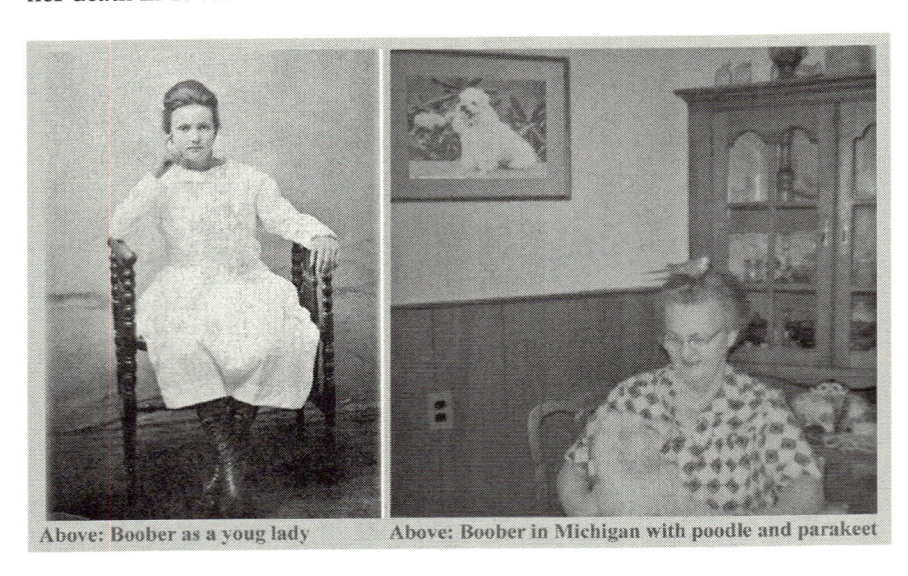

Above: Boober as a youg lady    Above: Boober in Michigan with poodle and parakeet

My mother's brothers who had migrated to Michigan, Vernon and Lowell, stayed there and married northern women. I remember visiting them when I was four-years-old. Uncle Lowell's family had a television, the first TV that I had seen. It was in a lounge area in their basement. I asked my mother if the room was a cave. My hometown of Marmaduke did not have houses with basements. In that room in Detroit, I watched Howdy Doody for the first time.

While in Detroit, my Uncle Lowell took me to a neighborhood bar, sat me on a high bar stool, and bought me my first beer. I took a sip or two, but as a four-year-old, I didn't like it. I think my uncle bought it for me so that he could finish drinking it, and have an excuse for exceeding his promised limit of one beer. A promise that he had made to my Aunt Betty.

Not too long after my family returned home from the Michigan trip, Lester Wycoff opened a television store in my hometown. My family went to his store to purchase one. Mr. Wycoff had a TV turned on with Rockette style dancing girls on the screen. That's the one I wanted. I thought if we had that set, I could see them dance all of the time. That's the one we bought. I still like TV and I did eventually develop a taste for beer.

**Marriage is Not Always Forever and a View From the Top of the World:** My great-uncle Floyd Ogles, unlike the vast majority of my family members, was married more than once. Members of my family in his generation did not divorce and rarely remarried even following the death of a spouse. Uncle Floyd was married eight times. Despite his many marriages, he only had one child, a girl, and she was by his first wife.

He was a very successful businessman who went from one venture to another. He always managed to come out on top. He was also a gambler, and a sporty dresser. At times he came across as a film-flam man. He had an enduring charm and was a family favorite. He wore lots of jewelry including a diamond ring that he won in a poker game. He passed down that ring to my father, and my father passed it down to me. I consider it a good luck charm.

I only knew the last two of my Uncle Floyd's wives. The one I knew the best was his next to last one, Luella. When I was a kid, my family and I would go visit Uncle Floyd and Aunt Luella. They lived in Dexter, Missouri, a town just north of the Missouri Bootheel.

Uncle Floyd and his first wife Gladys

Above left: Uncle Floyd's diamond ring
Above right: Drive-in movie screen

They owned a motel next to a drive-in-movie theater. Guests could sit on the patio at the motel, watch a movie, and hear the film's sound through a speaker that Uncle Floyd had arranged to be placed there.

My youngest sister and I loved to go to Dexter because we could spend the afternoon at the drive-in movie's playground that was located in front of the movie screen. The playground had swings, see-saws, and a merry-go-round. Duing one visit, I discovered a ladder behind the movie screen that went straight up to the top. I had to climb it. After reaching the top of the screen, I waved down to my sister who was sitting in one of the swings. I felt like I was on the top of the world.

My mama was helping Aunt Luella prepare lunch in my aunt and uncle's apartment at the motel. My mother looked out the kitchen window, and saw me waving from the top of the screen. My parents ran from the motel, screaming at me to slowly come down. I carefully descended while everyone held their breath. My punishment was that I did not get a piece of my Aunt Luella's lemon icebox pie. I never climbed the screen again.

**Boxcar Johnnie:** My great-uncle Johnnie Ogles and his wife Grace lived in a boxcar. He worked for the railroad, and when he was assigned to a new location, the railroad company would hitch his boxcar to a train and move it. The converted boxcar had all the comforts of a conventional home.

For several years my Uncle Johnnie and Aunt Grace had their boxcar parked in the town of Weiner, Arkansas. As a kid, I loved telling my friends that I had relatives living in Weiner. I liked saying the word "Weiner," thinking it was okay in this case to say a word that I thought was naughty. The town's name had nothing to do with hot dogs. It was known as the "Rice Capital of Arkansas."

When my Uncle Johnnie died, his body was sent to his hometown of Marmaduke. The funeral service was scheduled to be held at the Methodist Church with burial to follow in the family section in nearby Harvey's Chapel Cemetery. Uncle Johnnie's oldest sister, my grandmother, Eva Belle Harvey, lived in Marmaduke. The wake was held in her home. His body was laid out in the same room where my great-grandfather's body had been. All the mirrors were covered in black fabric. It was thought that if one saw themselves in a mirror with the corpse, they would be the next to die. The wake went on for three days. The kitchen and dining room were filled with food that was brought to the house of bereavement by friends of the family. A wreath of white flowers with black ribbon adorned the door.

At the time of Uncle Johnny's passing, I was 16 years-old. Once again I was experiencing the same wake and funeral rituals that occurred when my great-grandfather had passed away in 1959. Funeral and burial customs were set in stone. It was important that they were carried out properly.

On the first day of the wake, Aunt Grace confided in me something that I and the entire family already knew: she dipped snuff. In the early '60s it was no longer acceptable for a woman to dip even though a good many of the older women that I knew "dipped." Aunt Grace asked me if I would keep her secret. I assured her that I would. She then asked me to go next door to Mrs. Huckabee's and borrow some snuff for her.

For the next three days I was the secret snuff liaison. I would go to Miss Huckabee's house and she would wrap a pinch of the smokeless tobacco in a small piece of tin foil. I would meet Aunt Grace on the back porch, and place the little package in her hand. She would then retire to the bathroom for what she called her "alone time." I felt honored to be trusted to do this covert deed for my Aunt Grace in the hour of her need. We all want to be trusted, even if it is merely trusted to secretly deliver snuff.

Above: tombstone of Uncle Johnny and Aunt Grace

Left: Johnny Ogles

Below: boxcar

**Strong and Gentle**: My grandmother, Eva Belle Harvey, was born in 1893 in Big Sandy, Tennessee. To her family she was known as "Mom." She left Tennessee at the age of seven with her family in a covered wagon on their way to settle in Indian Territory. She didn't like the new land, was fearful of the Indians, and the wolves that often followed the wagon. She was glad when they left the territory and resettled in the Arkansas Delta.

When I was a kid, my grandmother lived on the edge of town in a house without indoor plumbing. Her source of water was a hand pump in the kitchen. The only source of heat was a potbellied stove in the living room. When I spent the night at her house, I would sleep in an unheated room in a feather bed. The minute that I awoke, my feet would hit the bedroom's cold linoleum floor, and I'd make a beeline for the living room to get to the stove. Mom did have electricity in her home, but there was only one electrical outlet in each room. Bare lightbulbs hung from a cord in the center of each room. She washed clothes with an old fashioned washboard, canned food, and preserved meat in a smokehouse. She cooked three meals a day on a wood cook stove.

Mom gave birth to eight children. The first two did not survive. She had an eighth grade education, and she never worked outside the home except for picking cotton.

Above: Eva Belle Harvey on her wedding day with husband Arzo Estus Harvey.

Above: Mom holding me in my family's front yard

One fall I was home from college for Thanksgiving break, Mom was sick. She had the flu. I insisted that she let me take her to the doctor. She didn't want to go. I asked her why and she said, " I'm afraid that he will give me a shot. I've only had one shot in my life and that was over 40 years ago when your Uncle Vernon was born.". I took her to the doctor, he gave her an injection, and she felt better. I sadly thought of all the physical pain that she had endured in her life without the benefit of numbing shots. Besides the pain of childbirth, she had suffered major burns as a child that scarred a large area of her body. She had survived many hardships.

It has been said, "What doesn't kill you, makes you stronger." Mom was the strongest person that I've ever known. She was also the kindest and most gentle person that I have ever known. I think of her often, but I miss her the most during the holidays. When she got older, every Christmas she would say, "I may not be here next year." And we all said, "Oh Mom, don't be silly." Then one Christmas she wasn't there.

**In the Garden:** My grandmother Eva Belle Harvey loved to garden. She raised vegetables to put food on the table, and she harvested enough bounty to fill the pantry with canned goods. In the summer her fingers were often stained different colors from handling the veggies. When she shelled bushels of purple hull peas, her fingers were a deep violet. She canned tomatoes, pickles, spiced-peaches, and she put up grape juice in fruit jars. In early spring and long before any fruit was ready to pick, she harvested some of the green unripe grapes and made a cobbler. The green grape cobbler had a nice sweet and sour flavor.

Even though she worked outdoors as much as she could, the only tan that she had was on her hands and where the sun hit her legs below her hemline. She didn't believe in wearing pants. She always gardened in a dress. Her gardening outfit included a cobbler's apron and a head covering. She generously shared her harvest with family and neighbors.

Mom could grow anything. Many times I saw her start a plant from a stem. She would spit on the stem's end, say something under her breath, and stick the stem into the ground. It grew into a thriving plant.

While vegetables fed her body, flowers nourished her soul. She had flowers all over her yard. She devoted two or three rows of her vegetable garden for growing flowers to be cut for indoor bouquets. She raised all her flowers from seed or from cuttings. She taught me to appreciate the beauty of flowers and I enjoyed working along beside her. One spring she set aside a small area of her garden just for me. We went to the store and I picked out zinnia seeds to plant in my section. I chose zinnias because of the many bright colors displayed on the seed package. The very next morning after planting the seeds, I walked the few blocks to her house to see my plants. They weren't up yet. My grandmother explained that it took a while, and she told me to be patient. She said, "Good things are worth waiting for." The wait was worth it.

One year she was given dozens of rose of sharon shrub seedlings. I helped her plant them all in a row on two sides of my parents' large yard. She said, "I think next to the iris, rose of sharon may be my favorite flower." I replied, "Mine too, next to zinnias."

Many years later when I moved to Fayetteville, my parents came to visit very early one spring and brought my grandmother with them to see my newly purchased house.

While my parents toured the house, my grandmother immediately went outside to look at my yard. By then she was in her eighties and had very poor eyesight. Looking out my living room window, I watched her explore the garden. My mother said, "We better go get her, she can't see good enough to keep from stepping on the plants." I said, "No, let her go." Having a few plants trampled didn't bother me. She explored the flower beds and viewed the plants as best she could. She plucked a little marigold, smelled it and held it close to her glasses. It was a joy for me to see her in my garden.

*My grandmother on the right, picking greens with her next door neighbor, Miss Huckabee, 1956*

She died a couple of years later. Every time I paint an iris, I think of her. In the spring I delight in seeing a pink rose bloom in my backyard on a bush that was started from a cutting that came from one of her rose bushes. In my front yard, I have iris blooming from tubers that a friend gave to her in 1944. I only wish that I knew what she said when she spit on a stem before sticking it in the ground. She had magic. At her funeral, as she had requested, the choir sang the old hymn, "In the Garden."

"I come to the garden alone, while the dew is still on the roses."

**Fabric of our life**: Everyone in our family and many of my friends called my grandmother "Mom." Mom grew up very poor. I think growing up poor not only taught her to "make do," but also taught her to "make." She could make a garden, make her clothes, make canned goods, but what I loved most that she made, were quilts.

Mom had a full-size quilting frame that hung from the ceiling that she used on occasion. Most of the time, she worked on a small frame that took up less space in the living room. She saved every scrap of material from numerous sewing projects, and family members and friends saved fabric scraps for her. She had dozens of patterns and enjoyed making quilts for gifts. She had a keen sense of color and design.

When I was a boy, Mom made a quilt for my bed. She let me pick out the pattern. I had recently bought a pet turtle from Woolworths so I chose a turtle pattern. Most of the time Mom used unbleached muslin on the bottom side of a quilt. For my quilt, she splurged and bought special fabric for the flip-side. The fabric was imprinted with red monkeys on a cream background. I felt "embraced" when sleeping under the turtle quilt.

Mom continued to give me quilts well into my adulthood. I ended up with more than a dozen. She gave the oldest that she had in her possession to me. It is one that she and her mother had made in the '20s. She also gave me the last quilt that she had made before her failing eyesight finally put a halt to her quilting.

The last one was a snake quilt. The pattern was not really snakes, but wavy lines of fabric weaving across the quilt top. On the backside she used a light blue fabric for the liner. She didn't have quite enough to finish the backside and had to use a little square of a darker shade of blue in one corner. She apologized for her mistake, and fretted because her final quilt wasn't perfect.

I told her that it was perfect to me and "Not everything has to be perfect to be beautiful." I loved it because she made it. It may be the favorite quilt in my collection.

Every quilt tells a story.

Above left: My grandmother, "Mom."
Above right: The oldest quilt in my collection that was made by Mom
Below left: Turtle quilt made for me by Mom when I was a child. Quilt had special monkey pattern fabric on the back.
Below right: Last quilt made by Mom. It is the snake pattern. On the backside is the dark blue patch she added after running out of the light blue.

**Sad Movies:** To family and friends my grandmother was known as "Mom." When she was in her '40s she left Marmaduke, Arkansas, where she had spent most of her life. She and my grandpa, Arzo Estus Harvey, relocated to Walnut Ridge, Arkansas. My grandpa had secured a job as a clerk in a dry goods store. All of their children were grown and out of the house except for a 14 year-old daughter, Billie Reba.

One Sunday Billie Reba asked if she could go to the movies. Mom thought it was not right to go to a movie on the Sabbath. She told her "No." Billie Reba instead went swimming in the Black River. Shortly after arriving at the river, she spotted a child drowning. Billie Reba was a strong swimmer. Without hesitation, she jumped into the river and pushed the child to safety. Then, Billie Reba was pulled under by a whirlpool. She drowned.

Mom and my grandpa were devastated. Shortly thereafter my grandpa, a man in his 40s, died of heart failure. The family said, "He died of a broken heart." Mom moved back to Marmaduke where she lived the rest of her life as a widow and each day relived a "what if" situation.

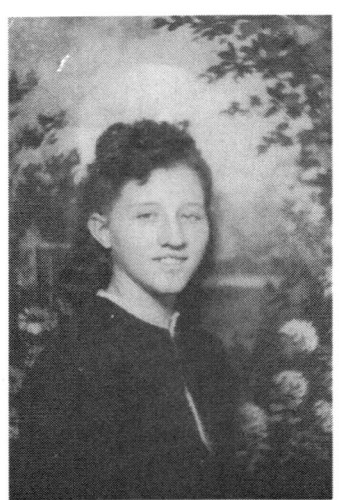

Left: Billie Reba Harvey
Upper Right, Mom in the middle, her mother, Vashti Ogles, on left, and her daughter Allene Taylor on right (my mother.)
Potrait right: Mom's husband, Arzo Estus Harvey, (my grandpa.)

Above: Mourner's at Billie Reba's gravesite.

After the death of Billie Reba, Mom would not go into a theater to see a movie, not just on Sundays, but on any day of the week. She would go with us on family outings to the drive-in movies, but she would not set foot inside a theater building.

In 1956 the Ten Commandments movie was released. My mother, Mom's daughter, convinced her that it was just fine to see that movie because it was a religious film. Mom finally consented to go and that seemed to be a turning point for her. I think she realized that she couldn't blame the movies, and more importantly, she should not blame herself for what had happened to Billie Reba.

While Mom lived in Walnut Ridge, a neighbor gave her some dwarf iris tubers. Although living there was a tragic period in her life, she loved flowers and could not leave that part of Walnut Ridge behind. When she returned to Marmaduke, she brought the iris tubers with her, and she planted them in her yard. She was very proud of them because, "No one in town had any like them."

In 1975 when I purchased my first home, she gave me some of the tubers. I've dug up and transplanted the tubers each time that I've moved. In the spring when they bloom I think of Billie Reba, and Mom, and I know in my heart that no matter what, "Life goes on."

**The Shawl:** Of my grandmother's fifteen grandchildren, I am the only one who she ever spanked. I deserved the spanking. I thought that her coffee table would make a great dance platform, but it proved not to be sturdy enough for the weight of an eight-year-old boy. One of the legs broke off, and I tumbled to the floor. Before I could get up, my grandmother grabbed me by the arm and swatted my behind a few times. We were both shocked and remorseful for what we had done. Oddly enough that event brought us closer, and we laughed about it often as she reminded me, "You were the only grandchild who I ever spanked."

My maternal grandmother, Eva Belle Harvey, lived a few blocks from my boyhood home. She came daily to our house to take care of me and my sisters while my parents were at work. We called her "Mom."

She had grown up poor and remained poor all of her life. In her later years she received a Social Security check each month in the amount of $66. She should have been eligible for the Commodity Supplemental Food Program. It was a government program that distributed food that included dried beans, rice, peanut butter, and cheese. However, Mom had managed to save two thousand dollars that she held in a special account to pay for her burial. If a person had more than a certain amount of money in the bank, they could not receive free government food supplements. My mother, Mom's daughter, offered to hide the money in her account, but Mom said that was not honest. She was honest to a fault.

Mom never learned to drive an automobile. When my family went somewhere, Mom went with us. She loved to go, even if it was just a trip to the Kroger's Grocery store that was in a nearby town.

Mom's five living children made certain that she had everything that she needed including a place to live, food, and money.

She loved and appreciated anything she received. She was overwhelmed by the amount of gifts that she received from her family on her birthday and at Christmas.

When she was a child at Christmas, usually the only gift she received was an orange. That was the only time each year during her childhood when she got to eat an "exotic fruit."

**Mom in her shawl, Christmas 1978**

One Christmas I gave her a transistor radio. She thought that was a very lavish gift, a magic box that played music without electricity. She often played it while sitting on her porch or while working in her garden.

After I was grown and no matter how far away I lived, I always returned to my parents' home for the Christmas holidays. Along with many relatives, Mom was always there. One year for Christmas I gave her a very dressy lace shawl. She loved it, put it on immediately, and said, "I'll wear this all day today, but then I'll put it up for good." "Putting up for good" meant to save something for a special occasion.

Before I left that Christmas, I was alone in my mother's living room with Mom. She was sitting in a chair still wearing the shawl. I took her picture and gave her a kiss. I made it to the kitchen before I broke down. My mother came to see what was wrong and I told her, "I'll never see Mom again."

I don't know how I knew, but I knew. She died three weeks later. When I went to the funeral home to view her body, I was touched and honored to see that she was wearing the shawl.

It had been "Put up for good."

**Throwing Stuff:** My father, Z. W. Taylor, was born in Tyronza, Arkansas, in 1914. He had attended three years of college before being drafted during WWII. After a stint in the military, he got a job as a school teacher. Although he didn't have a degree, three years of college was enough to allow him to teach high school. He taught math and etiquette.

After several years as a teacher, my father got a job as the manager of our town's bank. It was a small town branch and a one-man operation, he was also the teller and the janitor.

I often went to the bank at closing time to watch my father count the money. He did it with such speed that the cash looked like a green blur. My favorite part of closing time was watching him throw chemical floor sweep on the marble floor, and then watch him sweep it up with a large broom. Sometimes he would let me help. I had great fun throwing stuff onto the floor. I felt like I was getting away with something I shouldn't be doing.

While working in the bank, my father was robbed twice,. The first time was early one fall morning by a man who had my father put the cash in a cotton pick sack. That man was never caught.

The other time that he was robbed, four armed men came in and demanded cash. My father went back to the vault, closed the door and locked himself inside. Not able to get to my father, the robbers fled without the loot. My father pressed a button in the vault that activated an alarm in the drug store that was next door to the bank. The druggist called the police and they caught the robbers while they were fleeing down the highway. The druggist had the combination to the safe and freed Daddy from the vault. My mother was very relieved when my father quit working at the bank. As for me, I sure did miss throwing stuff on the floor.

**Big Daddy:** My father was a very large man. My sisters and I called my father "Daddy" until the day he died. I think that term is more commonly used in southern states, especially when used by grown children. My cousins from up north, called their paternal parent "Dad," or "Pop." My father was "Daddy" and still is when I speak or think of him.

Below: I'm being held by my father, Z.W. Taylor, Marmaduke, Arkansas

Z. W. Taylor was born in Tyronza, Arkansas. His father was a Methodist preacher. In my father's case, "the apple did fall far from the tree" when it came to religion. He resisted going to church and only did so for funerals, weddings, when his parents came to visit, or when we visited them. However, his "raising" did affect him in some ways. Although he was good at cursing and cussing, he never used the Lord's name in vain. That was an ingrained "no, no." He was a good person, just not a church goer.

Because his father's profession required frequent moves, Daddy lived in several towns in the Delta. In high school, he landed in Marmaduke, Arkansas, met and married my mother, and remained there for the rest of his life. Following high school graduation, he did attend Arkansas State in Jonesboro where he studied math and played football.

My father was reputed to be a very good football player. While in college, he and several of his friends went to a nearby carnival. One of the attractions at the carnival was a wrestling match that pitted a man against a very large live bear. After failed attempts by several of Daddy's friends to wrestle the animal, my father stepped into the ring and successfully won the match. His prize was $100, a large sum of money at the time.

Daddy had one year of college remaining when he was drafted into military service during WWII. After serving in the military, he taught school, and then managed a branch bank. In 1962 he was appointed to be the postmaster of our town, thanks in part to political pull and his friendship with Senator J. William Fulbright. Daddy's appointment certificate was hand-signed by President John F. Kennedy. While serving as postmaster, he also served a couple of terms as the town's mayor.

Of all his achievements, I think the greatest one was his role as a loving, supportive, encouraging, and understanding father. If asked when I was a kid, I think I would have said, "Wrestling a bear."

**Waste Not, Want Not:** My mother, Allene Taylor, was born in 1913, to Eva Belle and Arzo Harvey. Her family lived in the Arkansas Delta town of Marmaduke. They lived in poverty, but they were industrious and "made do."My mother was the oldest child. She had two brothers and two sisters. Her father worked as a clerk in a dry goods store, her mother worked at home, and they all worked in the cotton fields.

Left: My mother, Allene Taylor, in front of her childhood home, with her younger
sister and cousin. My mother is on the left.
Above: Allene Taylor in her kitchen.

As an adult my mother hesitated to throw anything away that she thought could possibly be of use. I attribute that to the fact she grew up poor, and she had lived through the Great Depression.

In the room that housed her washer and dryer, there were hundreds of plastic bags. Most came from Walmart, Kroger's, or the dollar store. Next to the stash of plastic bags were dozens of yellow margarine tubs with lids. In a shed behind the house, there were countless glass jars and cardboard boxes. In an adjacent shed there were dozens of small defunct appliances that included can openers, electric skillets, and coffee makers. When questioned as to why she was saving them, she replied, "In case I ever decide to get them fixed."

My mother was one of the sweetest people on Earth. This one little quirk, her need to save, did not bother me. It didn't border on real hoarding. It was just an effort on her part to not be wasteful. She did occasionally use some of the jars, plastic bags, and margarine tubs.

The "saving" did bother my younger sister, and when she visited my mother, she would sneak some of the stash into the garbage. She thought, "Mama won't miss this junk." My sister was wrong. My mother would call to let me know that my sister had thrown away some of her "stuff." My mother would go through the garbage and retrieve the discarded items.

One thing that did bother me about my mother's saving of items was when she put things up for good. "Putting things up for good," is a practice of saving items for special occasions. For my mother, those items were brand new and never used towels, wash clothes, nightgowns, and bathrobes. When I would visit, she put out new pristine towels for my use. However, in her towel cabinet were some of the most threadbare raggedy towels imaginable. She saved the perfect towels for use by company while she kept the raggedy ones for her own use.

Her "putting up for good" that I objected to the most, was that she saved nightclothes. My mother had a large old cedar chest at the foot of her bed. Inside were many brand new nightgowns and bathrobes. Most had been gifts to her. When I asked her why she didn't wear them, she answered, "I'm saving them in case I have to go to the hospital and then I'll have nice things to wear when visitors show up." I laughed while assuring her that if that situation occurred, I'd see to it that she was properly attired. In the meantime I told her, "Wear those nightgowns and enjoy." She too laughed at herself and said that she would, and she did. One Christmas I gave her a big fluffy bathrobe. I told her, "You can't have this if you're putting it up for good." We laughed again.

My mother was such a good person She only deserved the best. I tried to see that she had the best, even if it was just a bathrobe. Her idea to "waste not, want not" is not a bad rule to live by. And I confess, I do have some things that I've "put up for good."

**Tradition:** Because my birthday was on or near Thanksgiving day, my mother would bake a cake for me as part of our holiday dinner. Well into my 50s and as long as my mother was alive, I went home for that holiday, The family would gather for the Thanksgiving meal around the same dining table that was in the house when I had been a child. The table would be surrounded by various family members, and regardless of the number attending, my mother had more than enough food to feed an army.

Another family tradition was to begin shopping for Christmas gifts the day after Thanksgiving. My father on that day headed for the duck blind while the rest of us piled into the family car, and journeyed to Memphis to shop. We began our shopping spree at Sears before going downtown to Goldsmith's and Lowenstein's, both landmark department stores in the city.

Our holiday shopping spree took place long before the term "Black Friday" was coined. We would shop for hours, have a very late supper at Shoney's before leaving Memphis, and head back home in the dark.

For many years, I spent the Saturday that followed Thanksgiving day putting up my mother's Christmas tree.

Because the tree would remain up for a month, there was a danger of fire if the tree dried out. My mother often forgot to water it. I convinced her that it would be easier and safer to buy an artificial tree. We bought a fake tree at an after Christmas sale. The purchase took care of my concerns. We bought it at 75 per cent off and, my mother got to brag about getting it at "Such a price." She loved a bargain.

Mama had collected countless ornaments over the years. Many were handmade and were gifts from her beauty clients. When decorated it didn't matter whether the tree was artificial or alive. There was not a lot of green showing by the time I finished putting everything on it. The tree was in my mother's beauty shop, a large room that adjoined the rest of our house. Her customers spent lots of time looking at each and every ornament.

Every year my mother would tell me, "Everyone says it's the prettiest tree they've ever seen." She would tell them, "It should be. My son decorated it, and he's an artist." It was far from the truth that it was the prettiest tree ever. However, because it made my mother happy and proud, I too thought the tree was pretty.

I saw it through her eyes. She was looking at it with love.

**Steel Magnolias in Marmaduke:** My mother, Allene Taylor, was a hairdresser. Her parents, both with 8th grade educations, wanted my mother, their oldest child, to attend college. However, realizing that she had a passion for hairdressing, they agreed to send her to beauty school. The nearest beauty school was in Memphis. My mother's parents didn't think it proper for a young lady to live in a city unsupervised. They sent her to a cosmetology school in Birmingham, Alabama. She had two aunts and an uncle there who watched out for her. After completing the course, she opened Allene's Beauty Shop in Marmaduke, Arkansas, on Groundhog Day in 1935.

My mother secured a commercial space in the downtown area for her business. She paid $40 a month in rent. She and my father lived in the back area of the building behind a petition in what was essentially one room with a bed, a kitchenette, and a small bathroom. When my oldest sister was born in 1942, my parents decided they should buy a house and move the business to their residence. They purchased a home that was a couple of blocks from downtown. It was a large house built in 1900 with double parlors. They had managed to save the entire purchase price of $600, and they bought the home outright. They had a little extra money left above the purchase price. They used it to install plumbing and an indoor bathroom.

My mother used the front parlor as her beauty shop. She had built up a loyal and large clientele. Her customers in the little Delta town of 650 people included several personal close friends. During the early '70s some of her closest friends, Jean, Nettie, and Anna Faye, all decided they would each make their weekly standing appointments on Friday afternoons. My mother had one employee, Mavis, who was also a close friend. My mother would not take additional appointments on Friday afternoons. She reserved the time to spend only with Mavis, and her three friends.

During the Friday afternoon appointments while the women were getting their shampoo and sets, they shared laughter, gossip, snacks, coffee, and most importantly, friendship and support. The Friday afternoon get together went on for many years.

During the '70s my oldest sister was suffering from Crohn's disease. She spent many days in hospitals, and my mother would go with her during those stays. My mother's Friday afternoon friends always pitched in when she needed to be away. They cleaned her house and beauty shop, and made certain my father had supper. Mavis worked extra hours in the beauty shop.

In 1978 my sister at the age of 35 passed away. She died in one of my mother's bedrooms while my mother was working. The Friday afternoon beauty shop friends kept my mother propped up and smothered her with love, and helped her make it through those darkest of times. Their love and support ran deep.

As time went by, Anna Faye and Nettie passed away. Mavis retired in the early 90s. Jean was the last one still going to Allene's Beauty shop on Friday afternoons in 2002. That year my mother at the age of 88 was still working behind the chair. One cold January morning while she was dressing for work, her heart gave out. She passed away. She left the world still doing work that she loved, and she left with countless fond memories of Friday afternoons spent with friends.

Allene Taylor in her beauty shop.

Fifty year business anniversary, 1985. Pictured left to right: Nettie, Mavis, Jean, Anna Faye, and Allene.

**Looking Good all the Way to the End.** In the Upper Arkansas Delta, funerals are important events. Particularly among the older generation, there are time-honored funeral traditions with set guidelines, and with very little room for variation.

The traditions include visitation with the family at the funeral home usually with an open casket so the body can be viewed one last time. Prior to the funeral and during the wake, there is much socializing, and the bereaved family is gifted with enough home cooked food to feed the entire county.

The funeral service takes place the day after the visitation in either a funeral home or in a church. After the indoor service, a slow moving procession of mourners in cars with headlights beaming, follows the hearse to a cemetery for the graveside service.

When I was a kid, there was a woman who lived in town and enjoyed going to funerals. If there was not a funeral to attend for someone she knew, she would go to services for strangers. She would listen to the obituaries on the radio every morning. She attended any funeral that was within driving distance of her home. On average, she went to two or three funerals a week.

Women in my mother's beauty shop critiqued funerals with particular attention paid to how the body looked. The appearance of the body was important to them. They discussed whether or not the deceased looked "natural," and they talked about the dead person's clothing. "Did they have on their jewelry, and how did their hair look? Were there many flowers?"

My mother worked as a hairdresser for 67 years. During that time many of her customers passed away. At the request of the bereaved family, my mother would go to the funeral home and do the hair of the departed prior to their viewing. It was upsetting for my mother to style the hair of a dead person. However, she considered it an obligation to her customers. She wanted to make them look good one last time. Perhaps to lighten the situation a little, she would jokingly say, "At least I don't have to worry about how the back of their hair looks."

My mother knew exactly how she wanted her funeral. She planned every detail years before it took place. She wrote down the songs she wanted to be played. She made a list of the names of pallbearers along with an alternate list in case one or more of the preferred had proceeded her in death. She chose the color for the spray of flowers that would be on top of the casket. She prepaid for everything including the casket that she herself had selected. The only thing she did not pick out was what she would be wearing. She said to the family, "I might buy something prettier to wear between now and then, and y'all can choose."

The call came early one January morning in 2002. My mother at the age of 88 had died while she was getting dressed for work. I immediately packed and rushed across the state. I needed to be home. The family gathered the next morning at the funeral home to make arrangements. There was not much to do since my mother had taken care of everything. We did take a recently purchased outfit for her to wear. While making the arrangements, the undertaker asked, "And who do you want to do her hair?" I found myself saying, "I will do it." I had been styling her hair for years and I couldn't bear for anyone else to do it. I wanted her hair to look just right, and I knew that my mother would want it to be perfect. It was one of the hardest things I've ever done, but it was very important for me to do. I knew that it was the last thing that I could do for my mother.

She looked good.

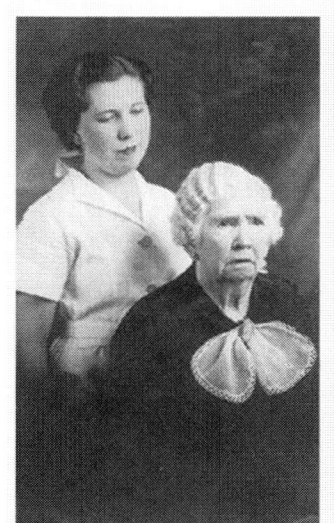

**Photo above left: In 1935 my mother started dressing hair. She gave this woman her first permanent wave. The woman was 90-years-old.
Above right: I'm with my mother, 1985, at a celebration of her 50th year as a hairdresser.**

**You Can Go Home Again:** My parents bought their first and only house in the early 1940s. The house in the Arkansas Delta town of Marmaduke sat on three big lots. It was one block from downtown in the little village of 650 people. The house had been built in 1900.

They paid $600 cash for the property. It took them a while to save that amount of money on my father's meager schoolteacher salary and my mother's earnings as a hairdresser. At the time she was doing shampoo and sets for 25 cents. It was a struggle for them to save a few hundred dollars.

Prior to purchasing the house, my parents rented a commercial space downtown where my mother had her beauty shop. They had living quarters in the rear of the building behind a partition. Their downtown space was small, and they had acquired very little furniture. When they moved into their newly purchased seven room house, it took them a while to furnish it. In addition to the price of the home, they had managed to save enough to install indoor plumbing in their new house. That allowed them to install an indoor bathroom, water in the kitchen, and a shampoo bowl in the front parlor where my mother had her beauty shop.

The house, like most in the Delta, sat on concrete piers rather than a slab or actual footings. During the summer months, the house was kept cool, or at least bearable, by a whole-house attic fan. The thirteen foot ceilings helped keep hot air aloft. Heat in the winter came from a floor furnace and strategically placed Warm Morning free standing stoves.

By the time I was born, my parents were well settled in their home. The house was in the middle of Marmaduke. It was an easy walk for me to go downtown and to school. It was also a good location for my childhood friends to gather. At night, the beauty shop became a teen hangout.

My parents always welcomed all who entered our home. My mother kept plenty of food and drink available to serve. My friends and I often messed up her kitchen when we cooked french fries or baked Chef Boy-ar-dee pizzas. My mother never complained about the mess or my frequent company. She knew if we were at home with friends that my sisters and I were safe. We were happy and content to be there.

I had my own bedroom at the rear of the house. I decorated it to my taste and changed the wall color every couple of years. After I left home and went to college, I knew that my room was still there. No matter my age, when I went back home, my room was a familiar refuge. While there, I was comfortably engulfed in a tender space where nothing changed. The same pictures hung on the walls, and the same knick-knacks sat on the dresser.

My mother lived in the house for 60 years. After she passed away, the property was bought by the Methodist church. They needed additional parking for the parishioners.

I vividly remember the last night that I slept there. I took pictures of every detail in the room with my mind, and I touched every knick-knack. I kept the items that were most important to me including a picture from a calendar that my mother had framed for me when I was five years-old. It now hangs in my current bedroom.

The church tore down the house. I've not been back to see the vacant lot where the house once stood. I do not plan to go back. However, I do not believe that "You can't go home again." I do. With fond memories I often visit the home that is forever in my heart.

**Boyhood home, Marmaduke, Arkansas**

Left: I'm with my older sister on the home's front porch

Right: Picture that hung in my bedroom during my childhood

# 5 FROM STUDENT TO TEACHER

**Cain't Talk Rite, Lik It or Not:** In the fall of 1964 at the age of seventeen, I enrolled in college at Arkansas State University. When selecting a major, I decided to combine my interest in art and journalism.

My dream job at the time was to be a graphic artist for a television station. I didn't realize that while studying broadcast journalism, I would be doing some on-air radio announcing. During my junior year of studies I was required to do an afternoon radio show each week that was one hour in length.

The news show was broadcast on the college radio station, KASU. My parents who lived 30 miles from the school were excited about hearing their son on the radio. They purchased a new FM radio so they could listen to my weekly show. The radio had a long telescoping antennae, and it had an honored place on the kitchen table where it sat for the next 40 years. At the time there were very few FM stations available compared to the large number of AM stations. Although my parents thought that their son was a radio star, I soon realized that I was not cut out for broadcasting. I found doing the show unnerving.

Reading the obituaries on air was particularly troubling. I was worried about mispronouncing names during a time of the deceased family's grief. However, I doubt that very few of the bereaved had FM radios. It was difficult for me to "talk right." For on-air announcers "talking right" meant speaking as if one hailed from the Mid-West. In the part of the Arkansas Delta where I grew up, the region was influenced culturally by its proximity to Memphis. That influence included the way we spoke. When outside the Delta, I avoided saying many words such as "bike," "like," "tire," and other words that I could not pronounce properly. Despite my pronunciation shortcomings, I did make a B in the broadcasting course.

Years later I ended up on air again. In 1980 I was contacted by the PBS show "Your Energy Dollar," about filming a segment in my house for a show about sun spaces. I owned a passive solar house with a sun space. The home was located a few miles outside Fayetteville, Arkansas.

As scheduled, the show's crew came to my home to shoot the segment. I didn't realize until they attached a mic to my shirt that I would be talking about the sun space. When I watched the show that aired later, it was the first time that I had heard myself speak on air. "Damn," I thought, "I sound just like Jimmy Carter!" I vowed that I would never be on air again.

Since that first television show, I have done more than 21 radio and television interviews. I also read stories for two "Tales From The South" shows that were heard by 130 million radio listeners worldwide, and I was featured on a StoryCorps segment on the Morning Edition public radio show that was heard by 50 million listeners nationwide.

I've learned to appreciate regional dialects, and I'm glad that we don't all sound alike. I have embraced my culture, and I have learned to accept the way that I talk. I now own my southern voice.
I rather like my accent......y'all.

Above: Home featured on PBS show, "Your Energy Dollar."

Right: I'm reading for "Tales From the South radio show."

**Not a Very Good Soldier:** When I attended Arkansas State University it was required that all male students take two years of Reserved Officer Training Corp (ROTC.) The four semesters of classes during the freshman and sophomore years counted as physical education hours.

Even though I had no intention of becoming an officer in the military, I had no choice but to sit through the classes and learn about modern warfare techniques. I was issued a military uniform complete with hat and black patent leather shoes. I was issued a rifle, and assigned to F Company. My company was jokingly referred to as "F Troop," a bungling military unit featured in a popular television show of the same name. The name was appropriate. We were the worst marching company on the field.

It was required that I keep my uniform and rifle in tip top shape and ready for inspection. I cleaned the gun and shined brass buttons and shoes each week before drill class. Although I thought I had fairly good coordination, I often dropped my rifle during the drills. F Company not only marched together, we sat together in the classroom. We were a unit, and were all given the same grade. One semester we all received a D, the only one that I ever made in my life. In actuality, I probably deserved an F.

During the spring semester all ROTC students were required to participate in a General Inspection, a dreaded affair when the Pentagon sent the big brass to ASU to inspect the troops. I was terrified about the inspection. The first year I didn't go. My sophomore year, an order was issued, "Attend the General Inspection or receive a failing grade." The only accepted reason to not attend was to have a written doctor's excuse.

The week before the big inspection and after having a few beers, I decided to go skinny dipping with friends in nearby Craighead Lake. Shortly after entering the water, I stepped on a broken bottle and ended up getting fourteen stitches in my foot. I was on crutches, had a wrapped foot, and I had a written doctor's excuse. Therefore, I did not have to go through the General Inspection. During the drill, I sat in the bleachers in my civilian clothes and watched the inspection. I was relieved that I was not on the field marching with my bungling company.

After two years of military studies, I had fulfilled my ROTC obligations. The following semesters to earn needed PE credits, I took tennis, bowling, ballroom, and choreography. I was a much better dancer than I was a soldier.

Cover of Arkansas State U Yearbook, my sophomore year

My Sophomore yearbook pic (A scrawny 110 pound soldier.)

Department of Military Science

ROTC Readies Army Officers

Interior pictures from ASU Yearbook (No, I'm not pictured as I was hardly a poster boy for ROTC.)

**White Skin and Fangs:** While attending Arkansas State University in the late sixties, when spring arrived I was ready to put down the books, get outside, bask in the sun, and turn my pasty white skin to a beautiful bronze.

In early April of my junior year, my roommate and I ventured to nearby Craighead Lake to soak up some rays. After we finished our morning classes, we loaded the car with a beer filled cooler, a picnic lunch, transistor radio, suntan lotion, and our tie-dyed hippie beach towels.

When we arrived at the lake, we found the beach area was crowded with sun lovers. We spread our towels in the grassy field near the water, opened a couple of beers, and plopped down to work on our tans. A short time later we heard screams. When we looked up, we were surprised to see many of our fellow sun worshipers running away from the lake and toward us. Then we saw them. There were dozens and dozens of cottonmouth snakes heading our way.

A large nest of snakes had broken up near the shoreline. Snakes often huddle together in a den to stay warm during the winter months while they conserve their energy until food becomes more abundant in the spring. The sight of the snake stampede was like viewing a scene from a horror movie.

My roommate and I left everything on the ground. We got on top of my car that was parked nearby. The two guys next to us did not move quickly enough and one was bitten. The young man who had not suffered a bite, asked us if we would watch their cooler and other belongings while he took his friend to the hospital. We said, "yes." They sped off leaving towels, cooler, and other belongings on the ground.

We sat on the hood of my car while we watched the snakes pass by us. The cooler with its contents of beer was not in reach. We sat there on the hood of my '59 Chevy, thirsty but too terrified to risk getting down from the car to grab a couple of cold ones. We stayed put long after the snakes had moved on. A couple of hours later, the unbitten student returned and reported that his friend had received anti-venom medication, but he was still in the hospital for observation. Still fearful, we got off of the car, loaded up, and made a hasty retreat.

I never again went to Craighead Lake.

Left: cottomouth also known as water moccasin.

Right: Craighead Lake near Jonesboro, Arkansas

**Hiding From the Wind**: Tornados appear quite often in the Arkansas Delta. The violent storms seem to thrive on the warm moist air and easily sweep across the flat landscape. My hometown of Marmaduke, Arkansas, has been hit several times. I was in high school when the town's warning siren went off to alert everyone that a tornado was heading our way. I was in the gym. Rather than seek shelter, I climbed to the top of the bleachers and watched the funnel cloud go by a few blocks away.

That tornado hit a nearby house trailer. A young woman who had been a classmate and had quit school to marry, was inside the trailer baking a chocolate cake when it hit. She was almost nine months pregnant at the time. The mobile home rolled several times before exploding. Debris from the trailer was scattered over an area of one square mile. Miraculously, the young woman was barely injured. She was taken to the emergency room, had a nail removed from her leg, and carried her baby another couple of weeks before she delivered a healthy child.

Marmaduke did suffer severe damage in 2006 when 200 to 300 homes were destroyed by a massive tornado. That was a very large number of homes flattened in the small town of 1200 folks. There were more than 40 injuries, but fortunately there were no fatalities.

My closest encounter with a tornado was in Jonesboro, Arkansas, in the spring of 1968, my senior year in college. An F-4 tornado ravaged much of the town, killing 34 and injuring more than 300. The twister hit less than one mile from my apartment. During the storm, it was pitch black, wind howling, rain falling, sirens going off, and no electricity. I heard sirens wailing all through the night.

Tornado, 2006, Marmaduke, AR. This photo was taken one block from my childhood home.

Aftermath of the 1968 Jonesboro tornado.

The next day a friend of mine called and asked if I would accompany him to the hardest hit area. My friend was a reporter for the local TV station. I would occasionally accompany him while he reported. I went with him to help carry his equipment. He didn't really need me to help, but we were friends, and we enjoyed each other's company. Going with him on assignment allowed me to get into places that only the press could go. This time I wish that I had said, "No." At the site, I saw things that I never wanted to see, and I have tried to erase the images from my mind. From then on, I only went with my friend to report on happy events.

The next assignment I helped him cover was a backstage interview with pop star Dionne Warwick. Images from the Warwick interview are the ones I try to hold in my mind from the spring of 1968. However, some things are hard to "unsee."

**Delta Politics:** Early on I learned how politics works. When I was thirteen-years-old I was standing with my father at the Marmaduke 4th of July picnic when he took a one-hundred-dollar bill out of his pocket and handed it to Governor Orval Faubus. My daddy said, "Sure wish that road between here and Lafe was paved." A half-dozen other men standing in the circle followed suit and each handed the governor a one-hundred-dollar bill. Faubus placed the "campaign contributions" into his pocket. Later that fall, the road was paved.

My father was a Democrat of the yellow dog variety as was everyone else in our town with the exception of one woman, Miss Lucy. When anyone mentioned her name they often followed it with "that Republican women." Miss Lucy was quite attractive and somewhat flamboyant. I personally thought she was quite glamorous. I was in her home several times and was very impressed with her decorating skills. Her bedroom walls were covered with yellow wallpaper that was splattered with big, bold, multi-colored flowers. Her bedspread and curtains had the exact same design. She had a bedroom like no other in town. She liked being different. I think that's why she was a Republican.

I turned 21 during my last year in college. I could then legally drink, and I could vote. The next spring, I volunteered to be a poll worker during a primary election. Miss Lucy was the only person who came to vote and requested a Republican ballot. In those days, ballots were tallied by hand after the polls closed. The poll workers, spent a lengthy time tallying the Democratic ballots. It took us a few seconds to tally Miss Lucy's Republican ballot. It was the only one.

My father was such a loyal Democrat that he could never under any circumstance vote for a Republican. In 1966 Winthrop Rockefeller ran for Governor against Democrat Justice Jim Johnson, a devout racist much like George Wallace. My father would not vote for a Republican, but he could not vote for a racist. Disgusted, he stayed home on voting day that year. It was the only time I remember him not voting. In 1966, only 11 percent of Arkansans considered themselves to be Republicans, but Arkansans were also tired of being labeled racist. Rockefeller won the election, the first Republican elected since the Reconstruction period following the Civil War.

My mother out of respect for my father also didn't cast a vote for governor in 1966. Shortly after the election she did tell me a secret. She said, "I have to confess that one time I voted for a Republican, but your Daddy can never know that I did." She continued, "I voted for Eisenhower."

I was shocked by her confession. I kept her secret. My father went to his grave never knowing that my mother had voted for a member of the GOP.

Some things are best left unknown especially when it comes to politics.

**Learning While Teaching:** After graduating from Arkansas State University, I pursued a teaching job in order to get an occupational deferment from the military draft. I was hired as a junior high art teacher in the Mountain Grove School District in Missouri.

I decided that if I was going to teach, I would go where the money was and at that time Missouri seemed to be the place. In 1968, the starting salary for teachers in Arkansas was $4,600. In Mountain Grove I was under contract to receive a yearly salary of $5,100. That amount seemed sufficient to warrant the purchase of a brand new '69 Chevrolet Camaro SS car. I wanted something cool to drive to work. The cost of the car was $3,600.

After taxes and teacher retirement were withdrawn from my check, I received $430 each month. For the first couple of weeks of each pay period, I felt rich. That was followed by two weeks of feeling poor. It took me a while to learn to manage my money. However, living was cheap in Mountain Grove. I had a roommate and we shared a furnished garage apartment, utilities paid, and the monthly rent was twenty-five dollars each.

There were not many places to spend money in town. There was one movie theater. The theater did not have heat and air. Moviegoers fanned in the summer and bundled up in the winter. I never went to the movies while living there. There was a liquor store. I spent part of my salary on beer. Most weekends were spent playing poker with fellow teachers.

During the time I taught there, the county where Mountain Grove was located was one of the five poorest counties per capita in the USA. The school district was huge and some of the students came from remote parts of the district. They would spend a couple of hours a day on a school bus. Some of the kids lived in homes with dirt floors. I had a friend who taught head start. She told me there had been times when she had to teach children how to use silverware. Not every student in the district was poor, but there was a disproportionate number who did live in poverty.

Due to the poverty in the district, the school received a large amount of supplemental government funding. I had art supplies in abundance.

I really did like the people of Mountain Grove. The students were very supportive of each other, and socioeconomic status seemed to make no difference to them when it came to clubs, cheer teams, and social groups.

It was a rewarding experience for me to be with them, and to experience their excitement and zest for living and learning. I too learned a lot that year. One thing that stuck with me is that "zest for living and learning is more important than money and possessions."

However, I do wish that I still had that '69 Camaro.

Yearbook, '69

Float that I designed for freshman class. I was their sponsor. We won 1st prize.

Yearbook picture.

Mountain Grove School.

**Poor in the Pocket, Rich in Experiences:** I was looking forward to Christmas break at the end of my first semester of teaching in Mountain Grove, Missouri. However, due to the poverty in the area, I did worry that some of the students wouldn't have much of a holiday.

Two weeks before the break, I decided to bring a little Christmas to the classroom. It was a fitting time to do 3-D origami construction, and have my 8th grade art class students make Christmas ornaments. One of the students volunteered to bring a cedar tree from his property and said that his daddy would deliver it in their truck. I bought a stand that night and the tree was delivered to the school the next day. It was perfect for displaying our handmade paper sculpture ornaments.

I had an abundance of white-as-snow velvet-like paper in my art supply closet. The paper was the perfect material for the ornaments. The students worked from two different patterns: a rose and a dove. The class had fun working with the paper while listening to Christmas music.

They enjoyed the easing of classroom rules while working on the project. I brought candy canes to hang on the tree. Not many made it to the tree. We ate them. While we worked on the project, we had a good time. I quit worrying that we were making excessive noise that may have disturbed the nearby classrooms. I made the decision that laughter was not noise, and that learning should be fun. No one complained. When the tree was finished, many teachers stopped by to admire the students' work.

On the last day of class before Christmas break, I let the students take home the ornaments. Many had penciled their initials on the white paper and knew exactly where on the tree they had placed their handmade decorations. They were proud of their work and I was proud of them.

I hope that some of my former students still have their ornaments and that somewhere a white rose or a white dove is hanging on one of their Christmas trees during the holidays. Most of all, I hope the former students have fond memories of a time when "We need a little Christmas, right this very minute" came to their classroom and all seemed right with the world.

**I Don't Like Math but I Love Figures:** When I was a young art student and I walked into my first figure drawing class, I was very uncomfortable. When the unclothed model took her first pose, I was flush and red in the face. It didn't take long before I got over being uncomfortable. I enjoyed the challenge of drawing the human body, and I soon realized the benefit of practicing figure drawing.

Each model presented a new challenge and my ability to draw improved. During countless sessions, I drew and painted all body types: female, male, tall, short, thin, heavy, black, white, duos, dancers, construction workers, and even a couple of very pregnant models. I thought each and every one was beautiful in his/her own way. That is until I encountered Breda. She was old.

My second teaching job was in Saint Louis. While living there, I took painting courses at Washington University. In one class, our subject matter was the human body. Breda was the instructor's favorite models. The first time she showed up to model, I thought, "Yuk, I don't want to see this old woman naked." Breda was seventy-something-years-old. As a twenty-two-year-old, I thought no way could anyone that old look good and be worthy of me spending my time drawing them. When Breda removed her robe, she revealed a potbelly, saggy flesh, and veins showing through her thin skin. I thought, "Okay, get over it and draw."

By the end of that first session, Breda had become my favorite model. Her body revealed great character, and I could sense the history of a lifetime of living. What I noticed more than anything is that Breda's gentle beautiful spirit shone through even though she was not saying anything, and she was sitting perfectly still. Her beauty radiated.

Painting of Breda

I was particularly drawn to her hands. They were somewhat gnarled with knotty joints, veins showing through, and with age spots. I loved her hands. Many people think the eyes tell a story, I thought and still think, "The hands tell the story and are a true reflection of a life lived. The older the hands, the more chapters that are revealed."

For the next two semesters, Breda was our only model. Most of the time she was nude, but at times she was would add accent accessories such as a large hat or feather boa. During breaks, Breda and I chatted and soon became good friends. Many times she would bring me homemade goodies. She was an excellent cookie baker.

I appreciate the time I spent with Breda. I learned a great deal. Not only did my drawing and painting skills improve, I learned that age has nothing to do with beauty. Beauty truly does come from the inside.

# 6 MEMPHIS

**Living Large While Living Poor:** In 1970 I gave up a teaching position, left Saint Louis, and went back to school at the Memphis College of Art. I wanted to further my education. I was particularly excited about painting classes. I wanted to get better with a brush. However, my choice to go back to school left me without steady income.

While attending the art school, I survived on very little money. The tuition at the school was $700 a semester. That was a lot of money at the time. When I had attended Arkansas State University a few years earlier, the cost of a semester was only $140.

My parents helped with the expenses and that included paying my $60 monthly apartment rent and the utility bills. The apartment was unfurnished. I did have a bedroom suite that my mother had bought for me when I was a child, and I had a black and white portable television. I had nothing else to put in my new digs.

My mother gave me several books of S&H Green stamps, enough to secure a metal bookcase, and to get a rolling baker's cart for the kitchen. I had one-hundred dollars in cash to furnish the rest of the apartment.

I went to the Royal Discount Furniture Store in downtown Memphis. I thought it would be a good place to shop not only because the prices were good, but because it was there that Elvis had bought the living room suite for his Jungle Room at Graceland. At that store, I purchased a $30 plastic studio couch, and a $30 dinette set.

After leaving the Royal Discount Furniture Store, I went to Barzizza Brothers, an import store. I bought a director's chair, some decorative dried grass fronds, and a large vase. I then bought curtains at Kent's Dollar Store, and returned to my apartment with two dollars in my pocket.

My mother faithfully sent me a ten dollar bill through the mail each week to spend on groceries. I could take that ten dollar bill to the Piggly Wiggly grocery store and buy a week's worth of groceries and still have a couple of dollars left to buy a beer or two during a weekend visit to a bar.

I ate lots of beans and rice. I was a vegetarian and often the beans were soy. They provided an excellent source of protein. I would cook a week's worth at a time. I blew the top off of my pressure cooker a couple of times. After spending hours cleaning beans off of the kitchen ceiling and cabinets, I finally did get the hang of using the cooker.

I had lived in Memphis for more than a year when I met Dick, a man who would become my life partner. He was a working man and he enjoyed sharing part of his weekly salary with me.

He earned $136.50 a week working as a bookkeeper in an auto parts store. That was good wages back then. Soon after our initial meeting, he started lavishing me with gifts that included a potted philodendron and a collection of Edgar Cayce books. I felt rather spoiled. Except for weekend visits to a local bar, we spent little money on entertainment. We passed free time while hanging with friends, sitting on the Mississippi River levee watching the barges go by, sunning in Overton Park, and exploring the city. We were easily entertained, but we were never bored.

One place in the city that we enjoyed visiting was Beale Street in downtown Memphis. In the early '70s, the street was somewhat seedy, and numerous pawns shops were located in the area. We only went to the area during daylight.

There was one major retail establishment on Beale Street, A. Schwab Dry Goods Store. It had been established in 1876. The store's motto was "If you can't find it at A. Schwab, you're probably better off without it!"

The store owners' never removed any of the merchandise from the shelves even if the products were from decades earlier. There were shelves stacked with hand written-sales receipts that had been in the store for decades.

I was intrigued by the store's voodoo items that included magical love potions, powders, and several kinds of blessing candles.

However, I was not convinced that spending my money to buy the "money" blessing candle would increase my income.

During one visit to Beale Street, I spotted a ring that I liked. It was in a pawn store window. It didn't matter to me that it had a plastic stone and was made from pot metal. I thought it was pretty.

Above: Ad for Piggly Wiggly, Memphis based grocery chain

Above: Early photo of A. Schwab store

Above: voodoo love potions.

Left: Cooking in my Memphis kitchen.
Above: My ring from a Beale Street pawn shop, 40-some-odd years after the purchase.

Dick insisted on buying it for me and happily paid the purchase price of five dollars, a sum equal to one-half my weekly allowance for food.

I still have the ring. The stone long ago clouded. It probably is now worth less than five dollars. However, to me it is priceless. It was purchased with love.

**Dancing in the Dark.** It was socially acceptable in the 1970s for two women to dance together. They danced together in nightclubs, street fairs, and even on telecasts of the popular American Bandstand show.

The same was not true for men dancing together. It was so taboo that when I lived in Memphis in the '70s, it was actually illegal for two men to dance together. I don't know if it was a city law or a state law, but it was one that was enforced in Memphis. Arrests did take place. Four male couples were arrested for dancing together at a bar called the Closet. The arrests were reported in the Memphis Commercial Appeal newspaper.

My partner Dick and I enjoyed dancing. On weekends we went to a bar called the Psych-Out on North Cleveland in Memphis. The bar closed at midnight on Saturday. However, no one left the bar at closing time. The tables were cleared from the center of the floor, doors were locked, and we would have a "private dance party." The cops were aware of what was happening inside the bar and would periodically show up.

The bar owner kept a lookout on duty and if the cops pulled into the bar's parking lot, lights inside the bar would flicker on and off. Everyone would quit dancing. By the time the cops were let in, we were all seated. After the cops left, everyone once again danced.

The popular '70s song, "Miss American Pie," was a favorite of the bar patrons. When that song played, everyone would stand together, place arms over shoulders, and form a huge circle. The circle, with up to 40 guys in the formation, would then go round and round in the bar. We whirled around the room for the entire length of the eight minute song, locked together, having a great time. We were young and reckless, and enjoying an activity that was perhaps made more exciting because it was illegal. We were brothers, arm in arm, sharing a secret that involved more than dancing.

We would dance all night long. At dawn, we left the bar, and several of us would go to the Ohman Inn, a diner on Union Ave, where we ate breakfast and made plans to do it all again the following weekend.

"While the sergeants played a marching tune, We all got up to dance."

Zeek Taylor

Dick Titus

**Wet and Wild:** In the early '70s while a student at the Memphis College of Art, I attended a lecture by Jimmy Driftwood. He was a famed folk singer and folk historian, who had written thousands of folk songs. He was most famous for his songs "The Battle of New Orleans," and "Tennessee Stud." He lived in Timbo, Arkansas, near Mountain View. Mountain View hosted a yearly folk festival each April. During his lectures, Mr. Driftwood invited college students to attend the festival.

Dick, two fellow art students, Linda and David, and I thought it would be a fun to attend the folk festival. We decided that the most cost effective way to make the trip was to camp out. Dick had an army surplus canvas tent that was large enough to accommodate the four of us. Linda and David had never camped and they were excited about experiencing a new adventure. I was also going to take my toy poodle Chelsea with us.

We prepared picnic food to avoid the expense of eating out. Dick owned a Coleman camping stove that we would use for cooking. The night before our trip, we loaded everything except the food into my pink '59 Chevy Impala.

The next morning when we were to leave Memphis, I could not find the car keys. Alas, the trip was off. Disappointed, I started unpacking. I had boiled a dozen eggs that I had wrapped in tin foil. When I unwrapped them, my keys were with the eggs. The trip was on once again.

Three hours later we were in the Ozark town of Mountain View. It was like stepping back in time. On the quaint square, there was music everywhere. There were fiddlers, banjo players, singers, and cloggers. Authentic hill music filled the air.

Along with hundreds of folk devotees, we spent a wonderful afternoon and evening enjoying the festival. Earlier that day, we had pitched our tent in a camping area at Sylamore Creek, five miles from town. We were joined by dozens of other campers. During the night while we were sleeping, the skies opened and heavy rains came. The small meandering creek in the park became a roaring river. The campground quickly flooded. Cars and tents were washed down the swollen creek. Fortunately, no lives were lost.

We had pitched our tent a little ways from the creek. Although we were spared the worst effects of the flood, we did get some water in our tent. The weather front that brought in the massive rains that April night, also ushered in unseasonably cold temperatures. The temps fell into the upper 30s. A brisk breeze created an even lower wind chill temperature. We abandoned the tent and took refuge in the car. After the rain stopped and daylight came, we loaded up our soggy belongings and moved into town.

We found a spot in downtown Mountain View behind a laundromat and pitched our tent. The laundromat was filled with folks washing their wet, muddy, clothes. The dryers were constantly in motion. We located our tent near the dryer vents at the rear of the building. Hot air blew in through the tent's front door. We were toasty warm. We celebrated our survival with a breakfast of hot oatmeal. Every now and then, we would venture into the laundromat to watch naked people barely covered by towels while they washed and dried their clothes.

Through it all, the music never stopped.

Above: Folk singers on Mountain View Square

Above right: My friend Linda Rosen, photography major, who documented our adventure. Above: 59 Chevy and tent. Right and below: eating oatmeal behind the laundromat.

Below: Dick, David, my dog Chelsea, and me on the town square.

**Oh Where Did That 28 Inch Waist Go:** While in art school in Memphis, I danced with Ballet South. George Latimer came to Memphis in the mid '60s from the San Francisco Ballet to work with the Memphis Civic Ballet. He was disappointed when he arrived to find that the Company was segregated. George left the Civic Company and formed Ballet South, and became its artistic director. He recruited African-Americans to be in the company. R&B singer Isaac Hayes was on the company's board of directors. The dance company was the first to be integrated in Memphis. I was proud to be a member of Ballet South.

Dance required a great deal of time. I had classes four nights a week, company class on Saturday, and rehearsals on Sunday. It was very rewarding and downright fun. Unlike the city's more traditional Civic Ballet Company, we not only did traditional ballets, we also did contemporary pieces. We would dance to Memphis music that included songs by Isaac Hayes, and by Elvis.

Ballet South was a semi-pro company. I would receive an occasional check. The pay was not steady. I realized that I couldn't depend on dance for my livelihood. Several of the folks that I danced with did go on to larger professional companies including the Atlanta Ballet, and the Dance Theater of Harlem. That wasn't in the cards for me. My professional path led me elsewhere.

I am thankful that I had the experience and I loved every minute of it with the exception of having to occasionally wear white tights. Physically, I was in my prime. I still enjoy dancing. As an older person, my plié is still spot on, but my relevé is not so good. What goes up must come down, but what goes down isn't always easy to get up.

**Summer Jobs:** After completing my first year of art school in Memphis, I found summer employment as a flower vendor working for a very laid-back hippie company. I sold carnations on a Street corner in Midtown. Each morning I went to the city's market warehouse district where I boarded a VW bus along with the other flower vendors. We were dropped off in various locations around town along with buckets filled with carnations.

I had a great spot on the corner of Parkway across from Overton Park. For each bucket full of carnations that I sold, I received seven dollars. There were about 30 flowers in each bucket and they sold for a buck each. I stood on the same corner every day for eight hours, and I was picked up at the end of the day by the VW bus. There was a gas station on my corner and the attendants were kind enough to let me use the restroom. However, each time I needed to go, I had to haul all of the heavy water-filled buckets into the restroom with me. I couldn't leave them on the corner unattended.

My second summer in Memphis, I worked as a prop person for the Memphis Summer Lyric Opera Theater at Memphis State. One of the shows that ran that summer was "Desert Song," a fun and campy musical that was set in the Sahara Desert.

The director decided that he wanted to have a live donkey in the show. The prop crew went to a farm in nearby Covington, Tennessee, to secure a donkey. Ironically, the guy that owned the donkey farm was named Mr. Burros. We had a trailer and loaded the donkey into it to take him to Memphis State for his stage debut. When we arrived, it was decided that I should ride the donkey into the building. All went fine until I rode the beast into the elevator where he started bucking for all that he was worth. I hung on for dear life, two floors up and two floors down. We promptly reloaded him into the trailer and took him back to Mr. Burros. The donkey was not in the show. There were no pictures of the incident, but there was a story about it in the Memphis Commercial Appeal newspaper.

In "Desert Song," the leading man played a Frenchman who also had a secret identity as an Arab Sheik, the Red Shadow. Not only was I the prop guy, I was also the dresser for the lead. He had many fast costume changes from Frenchman to sheik. I had a hell of a time getting his very tight knee-high boots off of him during the changes. I cussed a blue streak while trying to remove them. During the closing night cast party, I learned that the leading man in real life was a Church of Christ preacher. I think that because he valued my assistance, he never said a word about my cussing. However, I'm sure that I was the subject of many of his prayers.

**Where's the Beef:** While attending the Memphis College of Art in the early seventies, I was eager to explore alternative religions, philosophies, and lifestyles. I had been raised Methodist in a small town with a population of 650 people. Besides the Methodist Church, the town was home to four Baptist churches and one Church of Christ. In that setting, I think that Methodism may well have been considered an alternate religion. While the other churches practiced immersion, we were the only congregation in town that considered sprinkling to be an acceptable form of baptism.

While at art school, I became interested in Eastern Philosophy. Some of my "with it" student friends recommended that I read the "Autobiography of a Yogi." After reading and re-reading the book written by Paramhansa Yogananda, I was eager to give meditation a try.

Two friends of mine were certified instructors in Transcendental Meditation, a movement that was started by India native Maharishi Mahesh Yogi. Members of the musical group, The Beatles, were practicing TM. I was a huge fan and that was all the endorsement that I needed.

I had not known Dick for very long, but because I was eager to give TM a try, he decided to do the same. We were each given a mantra and began practicing meditation. As part of my spiritual journey, I decided to stop eating meat, and Dick went along with that decision. I wondered how my family would react to my new diet.

My mother was a great cook. Cooking was her way of creating, and serving others. When I told her I was a vegetarian, she eagerly began collecting veggie recipes, and she created meatless dishes to serve to me. She seemed to enjoy the challenge. My father never understood but never criticized. I'm not sure that my younger sister ever "got it." Shortly after Dick and I stopped eating meat, we were at her house for lunch. She served pork and beans. We said, "We can't eat that." She looked puzzled and asked, "Can't you just eat around the pork?"

Eating out became a challenge. At times, we ordered cheeseburgers and told the server to "hold the beef." I was often asked, "What do you eat?" I would reply, "Everything that you eat except for meat." Unless it involved eating a meal with someone, I didn't let anyone know that I was a vegetarian. It was easier than explaining the "why" and the "what," being judged, and many times being considered weird.

It was easier to eat at home. I cooked lots of rice and beans and kept a copy of the book "Diet for a Small Planet" on a counter in the kitchen. I followed the book's nutritional plan that combined certain foods in recipes that created complete protein.

One day Dick came home very excited and said, "I want to take you out to eat to this new place. You will not believe it."

The place was the newly opened Ranch House Café on Highland Avenue near Memphis State University. Upon entering, I couldn't believe what I was seeing: yards and yards of vegetables arranged for self-serve. It was the first salad bar in the Mid-South.

Many years later, I'm still a vegetarian, and I still get excited when I see a good salad bar.

**A Chance to be Saved**: In the early '70s I taught Junior High Art in Saint Louis. The people that I worked with became my running buddies. One of my friends, Evelyn, was a music teacher. Due to her position, she scored two free season tickets to the Saint Louis Symphony. I often went with her. I was appreciative of her generosity because as a poorly paid teacher, I could never have afforded to attend the symphony. However, there was a torturous trade-off. Evelyn had become involved in a charismatic Catholic-based faith healing movement. I had to feign interest and attend the healing sessions with her. I was not going to give up a free seat at the symphony even if I had to pretend to be interested in a religious activity that was somewhat strange to me.

The healing sessions would begin with the testimonies of believers who had been healed. There were always many nuns in attendance. I was a skeptic who was raised a Methodist. The teachings of the church of my childhood didn't include the belief in contemporary faith healing. We were prepared to take "what is" and limp all the way to the grave.

Despite being somewhat bored during the testimonies, I was fully awake when the star of the show took over. He was a priest, Father McNut, and the leader of the local movement. He was tall, dark, and handsome. He resembled a young Charleston Heston, and he was very charismatic. I think the combination of looks and charm gave him the edge to be persuasive. It didn't work on me. However, I kept going in order to keep in Evelyn's good graces. I wanted to keep my seat at the symphony.

After only one year in Saint Louis, I quit my job, and I moved to Tennessee. I enrolled in the Memphis College of Art to further my studies as a painter. I immediately took up a hippie persona, and vowed to never again wear a necktie. I let my hair grow long. I wore love beads and ragged bell bottoms. I was free.

I had been living in Memphis for about a year, when I received a call from Evelyn. She asked me to accompany her to a Kathryn Kuhlman event that was to take place in Memphis. Miss Kuhlman was a flamboyant and prominent faith healer with a huge following. Evelyn, Father McNut, and his followers had become groupies of the popular evangelist. I said, "Oh, what the heck, sure I'll go." Then I forgot all about it.

A couple of months later, Evelyn called early one Sunday morning to tell me that the day had arrived. She had saved me a seat to see Miss Kuhlman at the Assembly of God Church. It was a very large church, the one that Elvis attended when he was in town. When the phone rang that morning, I had just walked in the door from being out all night dancing, and I have to admit, I was still tripping on LSD. No excuse except that it was the '70s.

I was wearing a black see-through shirt, black and white striped bell bottoms, and platform shoes with stars painted on them ala Joe Cocker. I looked down at my clothes and thought, "Hey, these are good enough."

I jumped into my car and drove to the church. My friend Evelyn had ridden to Memphis from Saint Louis with a bus load of faithful followers of the Saint Louis charismatic Catholic movement. The group included a large number of nuns. I found my seat in the church and sat with my friend Evelyn and the sisters.

Fortunately, the row in front of me was also occupied by nuns. If I had sat behind one of the many women that were there with high hair, my view of the stage would have been blocked.

We were there early that morning in order to get a seat. We had to sit through the entire morning service while we waited for Miss Kuhlman's afternoon performance. For lunch we shared peanut butter and jelly sandwiches that Evelyn and the nuns had brought with them on the bus. By this time, I was really starting to suffer and was wondering if Miss Kuhlman might be able to heal a drug crash.

At one o'clock, Kathryn Kuhlman took to the stage wearing a very gauzy white dress and gold lame high heels. She was slender with bright red hair, and she was very theatrical. Shortly after she took the stage, folks lined up one by one to be healed.

Miss Kuhlman would describe the person's ailments to the audience, touch the afflicted on both sides of the neck, and they would immediately fall backwards into the hands of her attendants. If the attendants missed, the person would fall to the floor. They arose healed or so it appeared. Folks were falling all over the place on stage including some of the nuns from the bus. They fell to the floor like shot penguins.

As badly as I felt, I did find the healing service interesting and entertaining. However, if I had been a praying man, I would have prayed for the service to end. Two hours into the service, Miss Kuhlman called for all folks who needed to be saved to come down to the altar. I thought, "I have found my avenue of escape!" I got up from my seat and brushed past the many kind church goers and the nuns. They were patting me on the back, and congratulating me. They thought I was about to be saved. When I got to the end of the aisle, I made a beeline for the door, jumped in my car, and went home. I was far from healed.

I never heard from Evelyn again.

**Oceans Away:** My family rarely traveled. While I was still living at home, we did venture from Arkansas to Detroit a couple of times to visit relatives. Other than the trips to Michigan, we did not travel any farther than four hours from home. The other family vacations that I remember were to Hot Springs, Arkansas, Mountain View, Arkansas, and Lakeland, Tennessee.

While I enjoyed visiting those places, I really wanted to see the ocean. My parents and my grandparents had never been to the ocean. Finally, around the age of 16, I traveled with my aunt, uncle, and cousins to Virginia Beach and checked "seeing the ocean" off my list of things to do.

It was ten years later before I had an opportunity to go to the beach again. I was living in Memphis, had met Dick, and we planned a trip to Florida for our first real vacation together. We decided that it would be fun to camp on the beach.

Dick had an old pick-up truck. He rented a camper shell to place on the vehicle's bed to serve as our sleeping quarters. We loaded the truck and headed south to the Gulf. After several hours of driving we arrived at our destination, Fort Pickens campground on Santa Rosa Island near Pensacola, Florida. We got there just in time to set up camp before dark. We built a fire on the beach and relaxed in folding lawn chairs. It was then that Dick told me a story that put the fear of God in me.

A few weeks earlier, he had read the book "Jaws," and he proceeded to tell me the entire story. I kept glancing at the moonlit ocean and experienced fright akin to the fear that I had experienced as a boy scout while sitting around a campfire and listening to ghost stories.

Camper on truck | Zeek on beach | Dick on beach

The next morning after assurance from Dick that it was only a story, I put fear aside and waded into the gulf. After swimming for a while, we blew up our two man inflatable boat and ventured far out into the Gulf.

Dick manned the oars while I relaxed and looked down into the crystal clear water. I was fascinated by the sea life, especially the jellyfish that were swimming below us. Out of the corner of one eye, I saw large fins. I screamed. I panicked. I stood up in the small boat demanding that Dick head for shore. We almost capsized when I tried to grab the oars.

All the while Dick was laughing. He finally calmed me down enough to tell me that the very large, grey, leaping creatures with the fins were dolphins. I relaxed, but only slightly. I could still see them, and I insisted that we go ashore.

Even though I was traumatized by the experience, I still enjoy going to the beach. However, when I'm there, I'm always very cautious. I know somewhere out there is a shark waiting to eat me. Fear runs deep.

The written word is powerful and can change the way one views the world. Swim on.

**Trip to Bountiful, Uh, I Mean Branson:** During the early '70s, Dick and I took a three-day trip to the Ozarks during the Labor Day weekend. Our friends Joanie and Bonnie went with us. We left Memphis on the Friday afternoon before the holiday. Half of the citizens of Memphis left at the same time. Because of the heavy traffic, it took us an hour to get across the Mississippi River Bridge into Arkansas.

We drove for several hours before arriving in Branson, Missouri. We had not called ahead to make motel reservations. When we arrived in the "Country Music City of Mid-America," there were no vacancies to be found. We had no choice but to sleep in my '59 Chevy Impala car. We pulled into the parking lot of the Branson Walmart where we spent the night. The ladies slept inside the car. Dick and I bedded down in the trunk. We left the trunk lid open. The next morning Dick and I awoke very stiff, cold, and covered in dew. Dick had the serial number from the spare tire embedded into his face. He had used the spare for a pillow.

Zeek at the Basin Park Hotel

Dick at the Palace Hotel

After a day in Branson, we ventured South for our first trip to Eureka Springs, Arkansas. I immediately fell in love with the charming village. We had better luck acquiring lodging there. We found very reasonably priced accommodations at the Basin Park Hotel. The price was $10 a night per room. Dick and I had a room on the fifth floor. It was decorated with funky wallpaper and had a sink in the room. There was a toilet in a small adjoining room. However, there was no bathtub or shower in the room.

We discovered there was only one bathtub per floor. It was located down the hallway. We waited in line the next morning to bathe. Each guest cleaned the tub with a provided brush and comet before bathing. I hurried through my bath so others didn't have to wait too long. I emerged from the tub "clean enough."

A year later Dick and I returned to Eureka Springs. We stayed in the Palace Hotel on Spring Street and once again, the rates were $10 per night for two people. The setup in the Palace was about the same: sink and toilet provided with each room, but again there was no bath tub. However, bathing the next morning was a little easier than it had been when we stayed at the Basin Park Hotel. The Palace had a men's bath house in the basement. We were each provided with a luxurious oversized tub.

From the first time I visited Eureka Springs, I wanted to live there. It took years for my dream to become a reality. My house In Eureka Springs is on the town's historic loop, and is more than one-hundred-years-old. I'm happy to report, "My home has a private bathroom complete with a tub."

**Pretty Tree, Ugly Tree:** In the early '70s, money was tight and store bought Christmas tree ornaments were not in my budget. I decided that I could make ornaments. I strung popcorn and cranberries. I made stained-glass baked dough stars. I used a star shaped cookie cutter to get the shape. I then cut out a hole in the middle of the star shaped dough with a bottle cap. During the last couple of minutes of baking, I melted a lifesaver candy in the opening. I hung each of the stained glass stars on the tree in front of a light. When finished, I was pleased and proud of my tree.

The following December, I had a little money, and I bought some store bought tinsel and garland. I thought, "This year the tree will be prettier than ever." Dick and I went to a charity-based Christmas tree lot to buy the tree. For some reason and I can't recall why, we got into an argument while there. I huffed up and said, "I'm ready to go. Just pick out the ugliest damn tree here and let's go home."

That's exactly what he did. We took it back to my apartment. I was still angry. I put the tree into a stand and decorated it.

Tree with cookie ornaments. I have flour residue on my shirt from baking the cookies. I'm holding my dog, Chelsea

Dick with our "ugly tree."

It looked like a pitiful little shrub. I think the top had been broken out of the tree. It looked so funny that Dick and I started laughing and we soon forgot what the hell we had been mad about.

Every time that I looked at the tree, I smiled. It was a reminder of how senseless it had been to argue and fight. Although quite ugly, I think it may have been the best Christmas tree that I've ever had. It had meaning.

**Looking for Elvis:** The first song that ever made me cry was "Old Shep." It's a sad ballad about a dog that died, and it had been recorded by Elvis Presley in 1957. I was in elementary school when Elvis shot to stardom. My teenage sister became an obsessive fan of Presley. His fan base included women who loved him, men who wanted to be him, and people in all age groups. While hanging out in my mother's beauty shop, I noticed that her customer's conversations would often be about Elvis. His photo graced the covers of magazines that my mother's clients would read while they sat under the hair dryers. I anxiously awaited each issue of the National Enquirer. The tabloid newspaper reported the latest news about the rock star in every copy.

After Elvis bought Graceland, Ruby, a neighbor who lived across the street from my family, made a pilgrimage to his new home. When she returned, she had a fruit jar filled with grass that she had pulled from the mansion's lawn by reaching through the fence. Dick was friends with one of Graceland's decorators. He told Dick that Elvis had informed the decorating team that the ultimate decisions would be made by his mother. They gritted their teeth and let Miss Gladys Presley pick out things for the house. She thought that Sears was the ultimate place to shop, and many of the decorating items she selected came from that store.

One of my cousins met Elvis and had him autograph the top of her breasts. She liked to brag that, "He wrote "Elvis" on the righty, and "Presley" on the lefty."

During the early years of Presley's career, my mother gained several new male customers. At the time in Arkansas, it was against the law for men to go to a beauty shop, and likewise, for women to go to a barber shop. The guys who came to my mother's beauty shop didn't want to go to the barber where they knew they would be buzzed. They trusted my mother to leave their hair longer ala Elvis Presley. One client had my mother dye his hair the color of the King's hair. The men came to the beauty shop at night, shades were drawn, and the covert cuts would take place.

For several years, I continued to keep up with Presley's career and buy his music. I saw all of his movies. My favorite was "Blue Hawaii," and I saw it more than a dozen times. Alas, my interest and loyalty to Elvis faded with the arrival of the British Invasion. I became a devoted fan of the Beatles. I no longer wanted to be a southern rocker. I wanted to be hip and to be

English. I combed my hair forward instead of away from my face. However, when I moved to Memphis in the early '70s, my awareness and interest in Elvis returned. His influence was everywhere.

When he was in the city, everyone seemed to know. The Memphian movie theater was a few blocks from my apartment. If I drove by the theater and it said "closed" on the marquee, I knew that Presley had rented it for a private viewing. If the amusement park at the Fairgrounds was closed for an evening, Elvis had rented it so that he could take his daughter, Lisa Marie, on the rides. If he wanted to shop, his favorite Goldsmiths department store would reopen for him after closing to the public. The entire store staff would remain to wait on him.

His generosity to the people in Memphis was legendary. He was constantly buying cars for people. When my sister was in the hospital on Union Avenue in Memphis, Elvis was a patient on the same floor. He and my sister shared a nurse. The nurse excitedly told my sister, "Elvis, told me to go across the street to the Cadillac dealership and pick out a car." She did. He Paid.

I was sitting in a hotel room in San Diego when "breaking news' came on the television. Elvis had died. The year was 1977.

Two moves and several years later, I was invited to participate in a group art show that was to be held at the Arkansas Arts Center in Little Rock.

Above: I'm with Priscillia Presley
Below: my shrine to EP

Above: Not the real Elvis

The exhibition featured Eureka Springs artists. The theme of the show was "The Shrine." I didn't want to do a piece that was religious themed. I decided to pay homage to an entertainer who I thought had been deified. The obvious choice for me was Elvis.

Prior to creating the shrine, Dick and I made a pilgrimage to Graceland for inspiration, and to collect EP items from the many Elvis gift shops that were nearby. I used the purchased items in the creation of my art piece. I enjoyed visiting the Graceland mansion, and I think Miss Gladys did a fine job decorating. However, I don't think that "high kitsch" was what she had in mind when she picked out items from Sears.

I never did meet Elvis. The closest I came was meeting Priscilla Presley. That was almost as good.

**Yellow Nails and Barrel Curls.** After completing my studies at the Memphis College of Art, it was time for me to go back to work full-time. I had been a public school teacher, but I didn't want to return to that profession. I thought that it could be difficult to make money by selling art. My mother said to me, "I've always made a good living doing hair. Go to beauty school."

My mother had been a hairdresser all of her life. I grew up with a beauty shop attached to the house. I was very familiar with the profession. I thought, "What the heck?" and I enrolled in Jett's Beauty School in Memphis.

Precision hair cutting and blow drying were slowly coming into vogue. However, at school, most of the clients that we practiced on were still wearing teased hairstyles. We would rat that hair in place and spray the devil out of it. The school had a special pumping station connected to a vat of lacquer in the back room. Styling stations were connected to the vat with overhead tubing. A sprayer was located at each chair. The lacquer was very sticky, had a yellowish cast to it, and coated the floor, the chairs, as well as the client's hair. After a day at school, my fingernails were covered with yellow gunk. I scraped it off with a brillo pad.

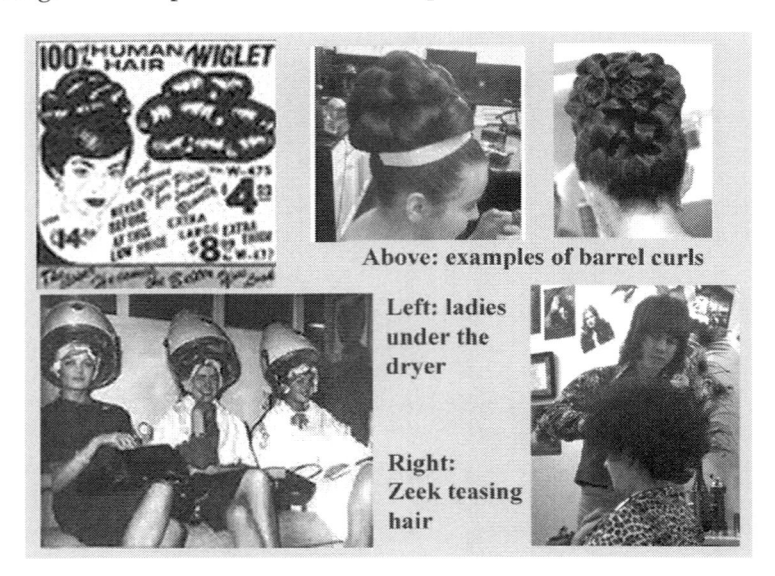

Above: examples of barrel curls

Left: ladies under the dryer

Right: Zeek teasing hair

Sue was one of my weekly standing appointments at the school, and she was one of my biggest challenges. She wanted her hair to be extremely high. When I first started doing Sue's hair, I thought, "I can't do this." She brought with her two wiglets, popular hairpieces at the time. Following the shampoo, set, and ratting of her hair, I would then put a teased wiglet on top of her "do." On top of that wiglet, I added another wiglet.

After doing her hair a couple of times, I changed my attitude. I began looking at it as if I were doing sculpture. I worked her hair and the wiglets into barrel curls, a popular style so named because the curls were big and round like barrels. One time I counted the number of bobbi pins that the style required. The count was forty-seven. Each week Sue sat in my styling chair while holding a Kleenex to her nose while I ratted away. I didn't know if she had allergies or if she was fearful of inhaling the lacquer that was floating in the air.

Sue was a small woman who weighed about 90 pounds. Her hair added another 12 inches in height to her small frame. Even though I personally thought she looked ridiculous, she often told me that she received many compliments from the women at her church. To them, Sue personified the saying, "The higher the hair, the closer to God."

**Karma:** After finishing beauty school, I managed a hair salon in Memphis. It was a Glemby Salon located in a Franklin Simon Department Store in Poplar Plaza. Besides managing, I also cut hair in a section of the salon called "The Cut Ups." As manager, I was in charge of hiring and firing.

Jean, a beautiful black woman applied for the position of hairdresser. At the time, black women were working in the salon, but they only were doing shampoos. The clientele of the Franklin Simon salon was 95% white. I liked Jean and wanted to hire her, but I didn't know if the white women salon clients would accept her as a hairdresser. It was during the '70s and it was the South. I contacted my boss who worked in Glemby corporate in New York and told him that I wanted to hire Jean. I wanted his advice and approval. He said to use my own judgment. I hired Jean. She proved to be a great hairdresser, and she quickly built a large client base. Everyone loved her.

A few months after hiring her, I was told by corporate that I needed to cut payroll. I had to let someone go. I had hired a couple of people after I had hired Jean. The person that I cut was the last hired, a woman who had been employed to do shampoos. The next thing I knew, there were two NAACP lawyers who came to the salon to question me. The woman that I had let go, had filed a racial discrimination suit. Jean overheard what was going on, stepped in with finger waving telling the lawyers, "This man does not have one prejudice bone in his body." And that was that. The lawyers left and never came back. Jean and I hugged and cried a little. I still love Jean, and I miss dancing the 'bump' with her. We were good together and we stood together. Karma does work.

**From Rags to Riches, at Least for a Day:** While working as a haircutter in Memphis, I was asked to do platform work at the National Hairdressers Association Annual Convention that was to be held in the Mid-South Coliseum. To do "platform work" a cutter was supposedly one of the best in the field. I don't know if that was the case with me, but I had received training as a precision haircutter in New York City, and in Philadelphia. Precision haircutting with scissors was the latest trend at the time.

I was flattered to be asked to demonstrate my skills as a platform artist, and I said, "Yes." As showtime neared, I thought, "What have I done?" I suddenly realized that the audience would be hairdressers and that they would know if I messed up.

The first day of the three-day show finally arrived. I was very nervous. The first couple of days I spent on the platform while I demonstrated cutting and styling techniques on models. I did this in front of hundreds of hairdressers that had come from many Midsouth towns. All went well, and no mistakes were made. My styles came out looking good, and the audience members seemed to be receptive and appreciative.

The third day of the convention was less about education. It was reserved for fun events that included a fashion show. At the time I was the beauty consultant for the Memphis Modeling Association. When I was asked to be a model in the show, I thought, "Hell, I know how to do this."

A few days prior to the show, I went to an exclusive men's store to be fitted with my modeling outfits. I arrived for the fitting in my "not-at-work" attire. I had on a ragged tie-dyed t-shirt, and ripped bell bottoms that had been hemmed with safety pins. I wore very nice clothes to work, but on my days off, I liked wearing my comfortable hippie clothes.

The snooty owner of the store was appalled at my attire and made no effort to hide his disdain. He said "out loud" some not so nice things about my clothes. If my mama would have heard, she would have grabbed him by the ear and given him a bad scolding for being rude. I didn't say anything. I was embarrassed.

One of the outfits that I was to model was a two-piece suit that was imported from Germany. It retailed for two-hundred dollars. I didn't know they made suits that cost that much. It fit me perfectly. I did proudly model the suit during the show. However, I was very nervous the entire time that I had it on. I was so worried about damaging the suit that I didn't dare to even sit down while wearing it.

After the show, the expensive German-made suit went back to the store. I never set foot in that exclusive men's shop again. I couldn't forget the comments about my clothes made by the shop's snooty owner during the fashion show fitting. No matter what he thought, I thought I looked just fine. At least, I was polite enough to know when to keep my mouth shut and to be mannerly. To me, that was much more important.

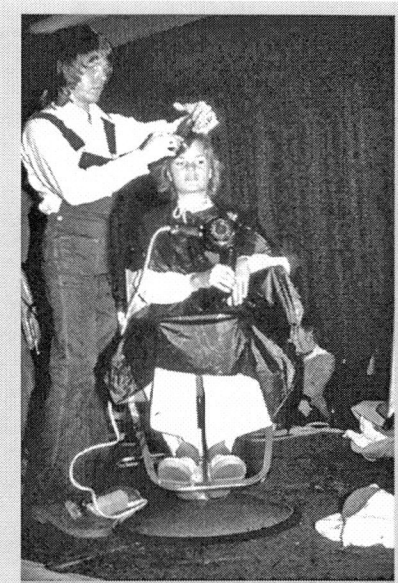

**Platform work**  **Modeling the $200 suit**

**I Can't Manage:** When I managed the Glemby Salon that was located in a Franklin Simon Department Store in Memphis, I was in charge of six employees. My district manager who lived in New York City, was impressed with my style of management. He offered me the manager's job at the Glemby Salon on 34th Street in Manhattan.

The Glemby Company flew me to New York and put me up in a hotel for a week so that I could visit the salon and consider the position. When I walked into the salon, I immediately noticed that there were six telephones and four receptionists. When introduced to the first receptionist, she asked, "Where are you from?" I answered, "Memphis." She asked, "That's somewhere out West isn't it?" I wanted to reply, "Don't they teach geography in New York?" but I thought it best to not be a smart aleck. They thought that I talked funny. I thought that they talked funny.

Upon entering the styling area, I saw a beehive of activity with 25 stylists, several shampoo girls, and eight or more manicurists. In an adjacent room, there was an exercise spa with six employees. I thought to myself, "They want me, a little southern boy, to manage all these New Yorkers."

I spent an interesting week in New York while considering the job opportunity. My district manager invited me to stay over a couple of days as a guest in his apartment in the Village. I said yes because I wanted the extra time to visit the city's art museums. When we got to his walk-up apartment and entered the living room, I thought how small it was. There was a door that I thought would go to the rest of the apartment. The door went to a tiny bathroom. There was not another room. In his one room, there was a roll up reed screen. Behind it was a small four burner cook stove, a refrigerator, a sink, a couple of cabinets, and twelve inches of countertop. His coffee table served as the kitchen table, and the sofa folded out into the bed.

He told me that he paid $400 a month for the tiny space. I thought that was outrageous since I was paying $60 a month for my apartment in Memphis, a space that was four times larger than his living space.

I decided there was no way I could live in such a tiny expensive apartment, and there was absolutely no way that I could manage all those northerners at the Glemby Salon in Manhattan.

I returned to Memphis, and I immediately made plans to move to Fayetteville, Arkansas, a town that better suited this southern boy. At least the folks there spoke the same language.

**Left: 34th ST, NYC**

**Below: Building that housed the Glemby Salon.**

**Left: Sporting a Glemby cut.**

# 7 FAYETTEVILLE

**MR. Toad and Company:** In 1974 I was managing a Glemby hair salon in Memphis, Tennessee. The salon was elegant, very modern, and was located on the top floor of a Franklin Simon department store. The clientele was upscale and required the latest cutting-edge styles. Several of my clients were local fashion models and I became the official beauty consultant for the Memphis Modeling Association. I felt that I needed to maintain a certain image at work, wear the right clothes, and that included wearing very uncomfortable Italian leather dress shoes. I was making good money. However, my inner hippie-artist child was screaming to be set free.

Dick and I decided to relocate to the Arkansas Ozarks. We chose Fayetteville, home of the University of Arkansas, to be our new hometown. The city's population at the time was 35,000. It appeared to be a charming place to live and work, with a more relaxed atmosphere, and a place where I could get by at work wearing comfortable shoes.

Following an exploratory trip to Fayetteville, I decided that I wanted to work in a hair cutting salon that was just off Dickson Street. A week later, I called for an interview, boarded a Frontier airplane at the Memphis airport, and flew back to Fayetteville to meet with the salon owner. I was picked up at the airport by a man in a chauffeur's hat and driving a long black limo. The limo belonged to the man who owned the salon and the chauffeur was his assistant.

When introduced to the staff, I immediately liked the employees. They were zany, offbeat, and they were kindred spirits. I got the job. The salon was named "Mr. Toad and Company" after the stylist who started the business. He went by the name "Toad." In contrast to the salon in Memphis, Mr. Toad's was a funky playhouse. The interior was filled with kitschy items and questionable collectibles. One styling chair had a sign on the back claiming that "Jayne Mansfield sat here." In actuality, she had not.

Weeks before I started working, the salon owner, who went by Dr. Johnny, ran ads in the local paper saying, "Zeek is Coming." People started asking him, "What's a Zeek?" He enjoyed the suspenseful build-up. The week that I arrived, an ad ran with my photo in it and revealed what a "Zeek" was. I was a little nervous thinking I couldn't live up to the build-up. When I did start to work, I was put at ease from day one and became good friends with my fellow stylists. We worked and played together, and laughed and cried together. We were family.

Although the original salon building has long been torn down, two moves later Mr. Toad and Company is still in existence. The salon has had more than one owner and as expected, multiple staff changes.

Sadly, half of the guys who I worked with back then are gone. Some perished due to the Aids epidemic. However, I'm still in touch with a few of my fellow workers from long ago. The move was a good one for me. I found good times, laughs, joy, and love. I found myself.

It is important to be among kindred spirits.

Above left: Mr Toad Billboard    Above right: Press photo for Toad ad and my "What was I thinking?" hair style.

**First Time Homeowners:** When Dick and I made the decision to move to Fayetteville, Arkansas, in 1975, I felt it was time to buy a house. A couple of weeks prior to the move, I boarded a Frontier plane, and flew to Fayetteville in search of our first home. Dick stayed behind in Memphis. He trusted me to find the perfect house. I had managed to save $4,400, an ample amount for a down payment.

The first day out with a real estate agent, I spotted a small house that had gone on the market that very day. It was a one-bedroom cottage that had been the caretaker's residence for an estate. The house sat on two huge tree covered lots and had a great view.

Nothing else mattered. I wanted it. I was unaware that the house had no value and was scheduled for demolition. The total price was $8,800, the value of the two lots. I made a full offer right away and beat out several developers who wanted the property. I took out a four-year loan on the remainder and my house payments were $145.75 a month.

A few weeks later, Dick and I loaded up our belongings into a U-Haul and left Memphis for Fayetteville. I was excited for Dick to see my real estate purchase. When he saw the house for the first time, he cried, not tears of joy, but because I had bought a shack for us to live in.

The previous owners who had lived there for many years were hoarders. They left everything in the house: stacks of newspapers, hundreds of glass jars, broken furniture, dead mice, and tons of trash. The former inhabitants were big drinkers of Pearl beer. There were hundreds of beer cans in the house and in the yard. The brick chimney in the middle of the house was filled with beer cans. The previous occupants were also big consumers of canned ham. There were hundreds of ham tins in the yard. They apparently had taken what remained in the tins out to the dogs.

There was one electrical outlet in the entire house, and a single lightbulb hung from the ceiling in each room. The walls were beaded board, and when bumped, the sawdust that had been used as insulation poured out of the cracks. The bathroom window swung out. The first time that I opened it, the entire window including the frame, fell onto the ground.

We called the city and they agreed to send garbage trucks directly to the home to remove the garbage. It took several loads. Following the clean-up, extensive remodeling began. We "paid" for the remodeling with hours of sweat equity.

We lived in the house for four years. By that time it was paid off and we sold it for almost four times the original purchase price. Even though we came out way ahead in the long run, Dick never again let me buy property without his approval. Thank goodness.

**First Home**

**View from living room**

**Some of the trash removed from the house**

**On the patio**

**The Journey Begins with One Step and Two Long Flights**: In 1979 Dick and I decided to take a dream vacation. We put back money each week and managed to save enough for an eight day visit to Hawaii.

When the day finally arrived to leave for the islands, we drove to the Tulsa airport, and boarded a plane for the first leg of the journey. We flew to Dallas to make our connecting flight only to discover that there was a problem with the huge 747 plane that we were to board. Travelers booked on the flight were split into two groups and placed on smaller planes. I thought, "Okay, this is fine. All that matters is getting there."

Take off in Dallas went smoothly. I enjoyed looking out the plane's window as we flew across the continent. When we approached the California coastline, land disappeared and I could see the vast Pacific Ocean. Hours later, we approached Hawaii. We did not land immediately because of a problem at the Honolulu airport. We spent more than an hour circling Oahu. I began to get airsick as we flew around and around. Finally, we were on the ground. I was wobbly, but I was happy when we entered the terminal. A pretty woman greeted me with a welcoming smile and a lei. I was finally on my dream island vacation.

The vacation was everything I had hoped it would be. We visited the islands of Oahu, Maui, and Hawaii. The last island that we visited was the Big Island. When we arrived at the airport in Hilo to board the Hawaiian Airlines plane for the return to Honolulu, there was once again a delay. We could not get on the escalator to board our plane. A child had sat down on the escalator and his buttocks were caught in the moving steps. I did not look and felt sick to my stomach. Finally, the poor lad was freed and we were able to make our flight.

When we arrived at the Honolulu airport, we were not allowed to board the plane. The incoming 747 from Dallas, the plane that was to take us back to the mainland, was stalled on the ground. The incoming flight had been threatened by a call-in bomb threat. The passengers disembarked, left their belongings on the plane, and a bomb squad complete with dogs searched the plane. After an hour-and-a-half search, no bomb was found. We were finally able to board.

We were among one-quarter of the passengers seated before the boarding was halted because a leak was found in the plane's hydraulic landing gear. We were not allowed to get off the plane. The plane's engines were not running, and they were required to run the air conditioners. We were hot. In an effort to keep us cool, not only physically, but in temperament, the flight attendants served free cocktails. By the time the problem was fixed two or three hours later, we were fairly tipsy. The rest of the passengers were allowed to board and we were finally airborne.

During the showing of the in-flight movie, "Matilda the Boxing Kangaroo," we were served supper. We were starving. I didn't receive my vegetarian meal as requested and therefore had very little to eat. I kept drinking. By the time our meal was finished, we had flown eastward into dawn. We had not had a "real" night and therefore no time to sleep.

When we landed in Tulsa, Dick and I were exhausted, and we were famished. We stopped at the first Oklahoma truck stop that we found and ate a late breakfast. While wearing leis and Hawaiian shirts and sporting a nice tan, we dined on scrambled eggs and toast while avoiding the stares of curious truck drivers. It was wonderful to have our feet on terra firma.

"A journey is like marriage. The certain way to be wrong is to think you control it." – John Steinbeck

**Rotel and Makeup:** In 1980 I decided it was time to go into business for myself, and I opened a salon near the University of Arkansas. Many of the clients were young professional women and sorority girls. To better serve the salon's customers, I decided to add makeup application to the services that were offered. I signed up for a three-day Redken makeup course that was to take place in Cincinnati, Ohio. One of the guys that worked for me also wanted to go to the seminar. We flew to Cincinnati on American Airlines out of Tulsa, Oklahoma.

During the next three days we attended the seminar. We learned "the art of applying makeup." The very last session was "makeup for men." I was sitting in the front row of the seminar that was attended by approximately 100 people. Because of my chosen seat, I was an easy target to be selected as a model. Although the makeup was very light, some foundation, a tiny bit of blush, and a light application of mascara, it felt strange on my face. Immediately after the male makeup session, we had to leave via cab for the airport. I didn't have time to wash off the makeup. When we got to the airport we had to run to catch our plane. I was very self-conscious about the "stuff" on my face. Even though my skin itched like crazy, I didn't dare touch my face for fear of smearing the make-up.

Shortly after taking off, the flight attendants came around, and to my surprise I knew them. The two women had attended the University of

Arkansas, and they had been clients of mine a couple of years earlier. Their regular route was from NYC to the Bahamas, but that weekend they had traded flights so they could land in Tulsa, visit Fayetteville, and pick up several cans of Rotel. They could not find that product in NYC. The attendants were craving Rotel dip, a delicious mixture of that canned concoction combined with melted Velveeta cheese. The lovely ladies immediately started plying my friend and me with cocktails free of charge. I soon forgot about the make-up on my face. By the time that we arrived in Tulsa, my friend and I were plowed.

Left: Zeek in front of salon
Above: Tulsa airport
Below: Rotel Dip ingredients.

After we retrieved my car at the airport, we stopped at the first restaurant that we came to, a 24 hour truck stop. I had to eat something and sober up before driving the two hours home to Fayetteville.

Before ordering, I visited the restroom, glanced in the mirror, and wondered, "What the heck was that black stuff that was smeared around one of my eyes?" I scrubbed my face until it was red. After that experience, I decided that I looked just fine with my face "au naturel."

**Ice, Ice Baby:** While living in Fayetteville, Dick and I enjoyed going to nearby Eureka Springs to celebrate New Year's Eve. Our place of choice was the Center Street Bar. It was "the" place to spend the holiday. Ignoring forecasts for bad weather, one New Year's Eve we drove to Eureka Springs, checked into a cheap motel, and prepared for our night out.

I was excited about a night of dancing, and I couldn't wait to put on my brand new shirt that was turquoise flannel with black stars. While we were getting ready, the freezing rain began to fall. Young and feeling invincible, we decided to go to the bar anyway. We made it there safely. However, only a handful of others were able to get there.

One group of people seemed a little out of place in the bar, four sanitation workers and their wives who were from Springdale, Arkansas. They were staying the night in the nearby Basin Park Hotel a location within walking distance to Center Street. The men wore cowboy boots, cowboy hats, and jeans. Their wives had on similar attire.

After a couple of drinks, we ended up sitting with the Springdale group laughing, and having a great time. Every so often Dick and I would dance. The Springdale couples also danced. They would get excited each time the DJ played a country song. Late evening and much to my surprise and to his wife's surprise, the burliest of the sanitation workers pulled me to my feet. Before I knew it, we were doing the Texas two-step to "Looking For Love." Even though I didn't know how to do the two-step, it was fairly easy to follow the big guy who picked me up and put me down where I needed to be. Dick was busy laughing.

That New Year's Eve was one of the most memorable for me. It proved that no matter our differences, by gosh, we can get along and celebrate life with any and all of our fellow human beings. We can have fun.

**Talking Slow While Wearing Flannel:** Dick and I built a home outside Fayetteville, Arkansas, and moved into it in 1980. I designed the house borrowing from several designs that I had found in magazines. The two of us did most of the labor even though we were both working full-time. After work, we would drive the few miles to the six acre building site and work into the night. I was under the impression that if I built a brand new house, I could have everything just the way I wanted it to be. I soon learned that budget restrictions put a limit on my plans.

Nevertheless, we ended up with a very nice three story passive solar house that was energy efficient. The home was entered by a forty foot wooden ramp that went from the street into the top floor where the living room and kitchen were located. The top floor was treetop level. An open wooden oak staircase led down to the other levels where there were two bedrooms, two baths, and a rec room. Off the front of the rec room on ground level was a sunspace complete with a hot tub and tropical plants. The sunspace served as a solar collector. When heat entered the room, the warm air was moved through an air system to other rooms in the house. The design of the house worked very well. The home was all electric and even during the coldest month the highest electric bill was $50.

During the early '80s there was a television series on the Arkansas PBS network, titled "Your Energy Dollar." The director of the show contacted me and asked if they could film the sunspace. I was flattered that he wanted

House at Weddington Woods

to feature the house on the show, and of course I said, "Yes." For days prior to the filming, I cleaned scrubbed, washed windows, and did everything I could to make sure the house was perfect.

When the film crew arrived they began setting up and planning the shots. I was very surprised when they wired me with a mic. I had no idea that I would be on film. The director said he wanted me to explain the workings of the sunspace, and tell how heat was collected and transported throughout the house. I was told to ad-lib my part and do so in a relaxed and casual manner. I was terrified. I was also thinking, "I wish I had spent more time on my hair, and I wish I had on something that looked better than this old flannel shirt."

The filming took a while. I felt totally inept during the taping of my television "show biz" debut. I thought that I was mumbling and stumbling incoherently. As time neared for the show to air, I again became nervous and apprehensive about the quality of my performance. My friends and family from across the state planned to watch the program. When the show aired, I thought the filming of the house was quite beautiful. However, I was quite shocked to hear myself speak with a slow southern drawl. I thought, "Damn, I sound just like Jimmy Carter." Over the years, I have accepted the way that I speak. It is part of who I am. I like listening to Mr. Carter. However, I don't want to be filmed in flannel ever again.

**Listening:** While living in Fayetteville, I became friends with Nancy Williams. Her husband was John Williams, an American author. He was best known for his novels "Stoner" and "Augustus." The latter won a U.S. National Book Award. In the literary world, that's like winning an Academy Award.

John and Nancy had moved to Fayetteville from Key West. She wanted to cook Cuban Black Beans and rice for me. It was a popular dish in Key West, but it was very foreign to me. I accepted her invitation to dinner. At the time I suffered from extreme shyness, and I was neurotically nervous about the dinner.

I arrived with a bottle of wine. I was not sure if the wine was appropriate. The clerk at the liquor store took a guess as to what wine should be served with black beans and rice. After arriving at their home, Nancy introduced me to John. She left the two of us alone in the living room while she finished dinner. Almost immediately he put me at ease. He was very humble and very curious about me, my background, picking cotton, and my general interests. I was flattered and no longer nervous.

That evening I learned a valuable lesson from him. Everyone has a story to tell if we take the time to listen. The best writers are also the best listeners. What I did not learn, "What wine goes with black beans and rice?"

**Going Public:** In the late '80s a merchandising representative for the Franklin Company of Chicago thought that my artwork would appeal to an international buying market. The rep who was also a friend, sold the company's limited-edition prints. Her territory was the entire state of Arkansas. She showed my work to corporate headquarters and they agreed to include my work in their line.

The Franklin Company besides having reps in each state, had showrooms in several markets from New York to California with the main locations in Dallas, Atlanta, and High Point, North Carolina. Shortly after my work was added to their line, I was asked to make a guest appearance in the Dallas World Trade Center showroom. I said, "I would love to." While driving on the way to the Dallas market, I started to panic.

During the personal appearance in the showroom I was to create a painting. The artwork would then be given away during a drawing at the close of each day that I was there. I had never performed as an artist in public with hundreds of people stopping to watch me work. I thought, "What if I messed up?" I was quite capable of destroying a painting with one bad brushstroke. I had ruined many a piece in the privacy of my studio.

The night before my first appearance, I did not sleep a wink. At daybreak I seriously considered getting back in my car and returning to Arkansas. However, I had committed to the task ahead and I felt that I needed to follow through with my obligation.

After a few brush strokes, while sitting at my watercolor desk in the showroom, everything seemed alright. I began to actually enjoy performing and visiting with potential customers. I breezed through the next couple of days and arrived back in Arkansas with a feeling of accomplishment.

I did a couple of follow-up appearances in Dallas, twice in Atlanta, and one time in High Point, North Carolina, I also made guest appearances in several Dillard's, a department store chain that carried my work. I'm happy that my parents taught me the importance of fulfilling obligations. I'm glad that I faced my fear of going public although my first time was nerve wracking, and best described by one of my Daddy's favorite sayings, "Nervous as a whore in church." Many of life's accomplishments begin with fear.

**7-Eleven**           **Silver Party**

**Too Warm in the 7-Eleven:** When I lived in Fayetteville during the late seventies, private parties dominated social activities. One winter, a friend well-known for his entertaining skills, hosted a party with a "Silver" theme. All the walls in his apartment were covered with aluminum foil. There were dozens of people attending the event, and most wore silver colored clothes. Alcohol flowed freely and folks were dancing and laughing.

One of the party goers, a very inebriated rotund guy, decided he was a "work of art." He removed all of his clothing and joined the folks on the dance floor. While dancing he exclaimed, "It's art, it's art."

Eventually he became tired of dancing and decided it was time to leave. Too drunk to get totally dressed, he put on his shoes and a coat that barely covered what should not be seen. He went out into the cold night air and took off in his car. We should never have let him leave. He ended up spending the night in jail.

On the way home that night, he stopped at a 7-Eleven to buy cigarettes. Before exiting the store, he went to the magazine display, spotted a Time magazine on the bottom shelf, and bent over to pick it up. That's when the manager called the police.

He needed a longer coat.

**Oreos Aren't Always Enough:** When I lived in the Arkansas Delta in the '50s and '60s, it rarely snowed. Most winters brought an average of one good snowfall. Three inches was considered a deep snow. The snow was rarely deep enough for sledding, and not too many kids had sleds. My older sister did have a wooden sled that my daddy had made for her. My younger sister and I used a piece of cardboard when we went sledding. The town had few hills. We mainly slid down ditch banks.

When it did snow, one treat that everyone seemed to enjoy was "snow ice-cream." The dish was made with freshly fallen snow, sugar, raw eggs, and vanilla flavoring. During one snowfall, a friend and I decided we could make the dish. We were at my friend's aunt's house. She was out of town. We searched through her cabinets and located all the ingredients. We knew what the recipe called for, but didn't know the "how much." All went well until we added the entire bottle of vanilla flavoring. We could tell by the color of the mix that something was wrong. No amount of added snow could make it right. The concoction went down the drain.

During my early twenties while living in Memphis, I only remember one good snow in all the years while I was there. The time it did snow, the city was at a standstill. I didn't dare drive on the slick streets. I was able to get around when the city cleared the main streets and the public transit buses ran limited routes.

My first contact with real winter weather occurred when I moved to Northwest Arkansas in 1975. Snows were more frequent and were much deeper than I had previously experienced.

A near blizzard occurred in North Central Arkansas in the early '80s. Dick and I left Fayetteville by car early afternoon on a Wednesday heading for my mother's house in Marmaduke, Arkansas, where we planned to spend the Thanksgiving holiday. We had planned to be at her house in time for supper. We usually made the trip in less than six hours.

About two-thirds of the way there, we stopped in Hardy, Arkansas, to fill up my Oldsmobile Omega with gas, use the restroom, and get a couple of cokes. Heavy snow began to fall. The snow had not been predicted.

We debated what to do and we decided to plow on thinking it would soon stop. A few miles outside Hardy, we came to a standstill. A quarter mile ahead of us, a semi-truck had jackknifed and blocked traffic. There were dozens of cars stalled in front of us. Very soon, there were dozens of cars lined up behind us. Nothing moved and the heavy snow kept falling.

Traveling with us were our pets, my little dog, Desiree, and our two cats, Josh and Priscilla. Fortunately, we had plenty of food and water for the animals. Dick and I each had a coke and we had a package of oreo cookies. We had enough gas to start the car every so often to run the heater.

The snow kept falling, and it got very dark as nighttime fell. Some folks became impatient. A driver in a four wheel drive pick-up decided he would go for it. He drove around everyone and veered onto the shoulder. His truck slid down a steep hill, and only stopped when it hit the tree line. We stayed put. We didn't know it at the time, but there was no snow in Marmaduke. I did know that my mother would be worried sick. A couple of hours after we should have arrived at her house, she called the state police. They knew nothing about the snowstorm. The police did tell her that they had received no fatality reports and that we were likely still alive.

We spent several hours sitting in the car while thirteen inches of snow piled up. At daylight, wreckers were finally able to move the semi, and the stranded cars ahead of us started to slowly move. By the time that we reached the next town, 30 minutes down the road, there was absolutely no snow on the ground. We had been trapped overnight in a very small freak blizzard. I stopped at the first phone booth and called my worried mother. She had sat up all night waiting in the kitchen with her radio turned on in case we tragically made the news. Two hours after the call, we finally reached her house.

We ate the supper that my mother had prepared for us the night before. It became our breakfast on that Thanksgiving morn. I was very thankful to be there. I made a mental note that when traveling in the winter, take more food on a trip besides oreos. However, it's still not a bad idea to include the cookies in the survival kit. When stranded, separating the layers helps to pass the time.

**Snow days in Arkansas**

Above: My mother in her kitchen by the radio.

Below: The location of the Thanksgiving snow adventure.

I'm in the snow with my sister. We are wearing car coats.

**Don't Dream It, Be It:** In 1975 the film "Rocky Horror Picture Show" hit the theaters and instantly became a cult classic. I was obsessed with the movie and saw it many times. Before the movie was released on disc, I had received a bootleg copy recorded during a movie screening. As poor as that copy was, I was thrilled to have it and played it over and over.

I didn't think about why I and others were so obsessed with the rather bizarre musical. Granted the songs were top-notch, but I do think the movie's appeal went far beyond the score. Perhaps the movie said to us, "It's quite all right to celebrate who you are, and have fun. Don't Dream it, Be It."

In the mid '80s the movie, "Pass the Ammo," was being filmed in Eureka Springs. The film starred Tom Paxton, Annie Potts, Linda Kozlowski, and Tim Curry. Although all the actors were fairly well known, Annie Potts for Designing Women, Linda Kozlowski for Crocodile Dundee, and Tom Paxton for many roles, I only cared that Tim Curry was in Arkansas. He had played Dr. Frank-N-Furter in Rocky Horror.

I was still living in Fayetteville during the filming. My "stalking" of Mr. Curry required that I drive to Eureka Springs in hopes of spotting Tim. I was determined to meet him. My determination paid off when late one evening, I spotted him in front of the post office in the company of Annie Potts and Linda Kozlowski. I slammed on the brakes, jumped out of the car, and ran toward them with the "Rocky Horror Picture Show" book in my hand. Unfortunately in my haste, I somewhat pushed the actresses aside in order to get to Mr. Curry.

He was very gracious, and he was pleased that I had the book. He called it "The bloody Rocky Horror Bible," and he was nice enough to sign it. I still cherish that autograph and I still appreciate the effect the movie had on me. It relayed a positive message to me and to many others. We needed to know that it was okay "to be different." Annie Potts and Linda Kozlowski, please forgive me for almost knocking you down.

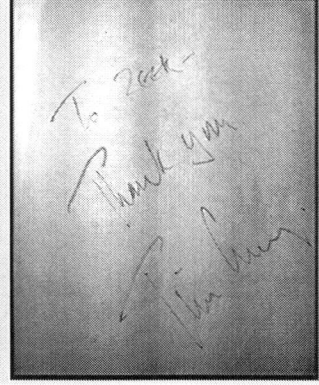

**Walk On By:** When Dick and I lived in Fayetteville from 1975 until 1987, he worked in the trades. He was as an electrician. He worked on job sites with men who were carpenters, plumbers, concrete finishers, and other types of construction workers. They did not know that Dick was gay and he wanted that part of "who he is" to remain a secret. He did not want them to know for various reasons: scorn, ridicule, rejection, and the fear of being fired.

Dick's given name is Oscar Dickerson. To friends and family he is known as "Dick." When at work, he went by "Oscar." If we were in public together, we had signals. If we were walking together on the street or at the mall and someone said "Hey Oscar," I knew it was someone from work greeting him. I would keep on walking and at that moment we became strangers. After he finished talking to his fellow workman, we would again link up and go about our business together.

During that time, we had two houses. We lived in one. Dick kept the other one furnished, kept the utilities connected, and stocked the refrigerator with beer. If a man from work wanted to stop by at the end of the day for a beer, Dick met him at the spare house. There were two separate houses and two separate lives that we created because we feared everyone would know that we were gay. We feared.

In 1987 we moved to Eureka Springs, Dick was working for himself. We felt safe, and we felt comfortable being known as a couple. We felt accepted for who we are, and we decided there would be no more hiding. We would have one house and one life together. My hope is that from this time forward, no one will ever have to live in fear because of who they are, and who they love.

I hope that there will never again be a need to "Walk on by."

# 8. EUREKA SPRINGS

**Following My Heart:** The first time that I visited Eureka Springs, Arkansas, I felt the magic. In the early '70s, Dick and I vacationed in the resort town located in the Ozark Mountains. I was drawn to the natural scenic beauty, the Victorian architecture, and particularly the town's funkiness. The village was unlike any place that I had been during my travels. I was envious of the hippies, artists, gays, and free spirits, who were privileged to live there. I wanted to live there too.

There was a problem. The little town's economy was not too good. Some of the buildings were boarded up . I didn't see the potential for me to earn a living as a hair cutter. In 1975 Dick and I moved to Fayetteville, Arkansas, home to the state's largest university. The larger town with a big student population was a ripe market for me to practice the latest trend of hair styling: precision scissor cutting and blow drying. I had been trained in those styling techniques during classes in Philadelphia and New York City.

I enjoyed living in Fayetteville. I earned a good living there, and I made many good friends in the city. While there I also continued to pursue my other profession. I worked diligently to become a better artist. I did shows, and I exhibited in galleries. I was able to get my work sold on the national market, and eventually my art became my main source of income.

By the late '80s Eureka Springs had boomed, especially the town's art scene. After thirteen years in Fayetteville, I was able to relocate to Eureka Springs. I did leave a part of my heart in Fayetteville. Fortunately the towns are only one hour apart. I consider them to be "hometown one" and "hometown two."

It was good luck or perhaps fate that I bought a house on White Street in Eureka Springs. It is on the Upper Historic Loop, and the street is home to many artists. Two of the artists, Mary Springer and Eleanor Lux, ironically had also gone to the Memphis College of Art, the same school that I had attended. Together we established the "White Street Studio Walk," an annual art show that has been going on for more than a quarter century.

I can walk out onto my front porch, look in any direction, and see the home or the studio of an artist. I followed my heart, stuck to my dream, and found my tribe. I found "home."

Right: My house on White ST.

**The Party Has to End Sometime:** My friend Lester Armagost loved Halloween. He lived around the corner from me in a turn of the century house. In mid-October Lester would start turning his house into a haunted castle. For many years, it was the location for the town's most popular and much anticipated Halloween party. The prep involved removing furniture from the lower floor, stapling Visqueen to the walls, putting up decorations, and hauling in bales of hay for seating. For the yearly party, Lester did things to his house that most folks would never consider doing.

On Halloween night, Lester would open his home to the children who were trick or treating. Later in the evening at 9 o'clock, the house was open to adults. During the Halloween party the upstairs bathtub served as an iced beer bin. There was a well-stocked bar in his kitchen. Lester hired bartenders to mix drinks. He did everything necessary to create a good time for his guests.

I knew Lester was ill before we met and became friends. That didn't bother me. I knew several people who had AIDS. I had lost friends to the disease. When I lived in Fayetteville I hung out with four guys who I considered my best friends. Of the four, three succumbed to the disease. Although there was a fear among the general population, I knew that AIDS could not be transmitted through casual contact. The stupid disease was not going to keep me from making and loving friends, sick or not.

During March of 1994, a late season snowstorm dropped several inches of snow on Eureka Springs. Lester called to tell me that we had a friend, Steve, who was in bad shape, and was in the ICU at the Eureka Springs hospital. Because the roads were impassable Steve's nearest relative, a brother living in Oklahoma, could not travel to Eureka Springs to be with Steve. Lester and I donned our snow boots and walked to the hospital. We didn't want our friend to be alone.

Even though we weren't really family because of the seriousness of Steve's situation, the staff bent the rules. They let us sit in the ICU with Steve. I don't know if Steve knew we were there, but I like to think that he did know. Lester and I would rub his arms and legs, and hold his hand.

As sad and trying as the situation was for Lester and me, the time the two of us spent together at the hospital sitting with Steve was quality time. We cried, we laughed, and we talked about friendship, hopes, and fears. I kept thinking that it could be Lester in that bed. Lester was thinking the same. Steve lived less than 24 hours after being admitted. He was 39-years-old when he passed. Before leaving the hospital, Lester and I had a good cry, hugged for a long time, and silently walked home in the snow.

The weather in July of 1995 was summer-time hot when Lester became bedridden. Unlike Steve who passed in a hospital, Lester was in a bed in his home, and surrounded by many friends who sat with him during his final hours. He lay unconscious with flowers strewn all around him on the bed and pillow. I was very sad. At the same time, I thought that the sight of him on the bed, smothered in flowers like an Indian prince, was beautiful. I knew that Lester was surrounded by love when he left us. He died at the age of forty-one.

The following Halloween, there was one more party in Lester's house. The party was held to honor him and it was as festive and as much fun as ever. Lester would have liked that. His ashes were at the party in a beautiful urn and I know he was there in spirit.

It is good to leave this world while being loved.

Lester Armagost

**Mardi Gras, the Good Times Rolled:** In 1995, I attended my first Mardi Gras when Dick and I visited friends who were living on Magazine Street in New Orleans. Their apartment was in easy walking distance to the famous French Quarter and to Canal Street, the location of numerous Mardi Gras parades.

One of our hosts, was a regional manager of several McDonalds restaurants in the metro area. Two of the restaurants faced Canal and each had a second story balcony. The balconies provided perfect viewing spots for parade watching and saved us from being lost in the madness of the crowds on the street. Many of the floats were two stories tall, and because we were watching from a two-story balcony, we were easy targets for bead tossers. We collected lots of beads and trinkets thrown to us on our lofty perch. Actor John Larroquette served as the monarch of the Krewe of Bacchus parade that year and he easily tossed some gold beads to me.

My New Orleans friend was a member of a daiquiri club. Late each day while we were there, two gallons of frozen daiquiris were delivered to the McDonald's restaurant on the corner of Canal and Royal. We enjoyed sitting on the balcony, sipping cocktails, and watching the revelry below.

The first night after arriving in New Orleans, we spent hours partying in the quarter. We partied way too much, and tried unsuccessfully to keep each other standing. Dick, one of my friends, and I pulled each other down into a nasty gutter. I thought my clothes were ruined. After that fall, I was very careful to remain standing at all cost.

In between parades, we strolled around the Quarter, and spent many hours on Bourbon Street. I was shocked at what folks would do to get cheap plastic beads thrown to them. Vendors were selling big cans of beer for one dollar. The beers were cooled in garbage cans filled with ice that were sitting directly on the sidewalk. I thought, "Man, this is living."

**McDonalds, NOLA**    **Payless Shoes**    **King Krazo, 2009**

The downside to the consumption of many beers was frequently needing to use a restroom. We kept running back to McDonalds because we knew our friend working there would let us use the restaurant's bathroom. The other option was waiting in line to use porta-potties that were sitting in urine soaked mud. Entering required walking a wooden plank that had been placed over the mud pit. Squirming on the way to McDonald's seemed to be the better option.

The day after Mardi Gras ended, Dick and I walked to Payless shoes, bought new shoes, and left our "party" shoes on top of a Times Picayune newspaper machine. We hoped a homeless person could clean the shoes and get some use out of them. We didn't dare enter our car wearing the shoes that had walked the streets during Mardi Gras. They had waded through garbage and unspeakable waste created by thousands of revelers.

Years later in 2009, I was honored to be King Krazo during the Eureka Springs Mardi Gras. Although much less decadent than the Mardi Gras in New Orleans, I had just as much fun celebrating the holiday in my hometown, and I didn't have to throw away my shoes.

**Shake, Rattle and Roll....Not:** The Arkansas Delta is located in the New Madrid Earthquake Zone. The zone runs approximately 125 miles from Cairo, Illinois, all the way to Mark Tree, Arkansas. The potential quake area includes five states. According to scientists, the area is long overdue for occurrence of another major quake.

In the winter of 1811-1812 there were three to five major quakes in the area with the epicenter in New Madrid, Missouri. Because there were very few European settlers in the area, there were few structures in place that were destroyed. It was reported during the quakes that church bells rang from the shaking as far away as Boston. The Mississippi River ran backwards for three days and the back flow created Reelfoot Lake in Northwest Tennessee.

While growing up in the Delta, I felt occasional tremors and I experienced ground shaking while living in Memphis. While living in Eureka Springs, the only time I thought about earthquakes was when I returned to the Delta. The possibility of the New Madrid Fault becoming active was foremost on my mind each time I was on the bridge spanning the Mississippi River between Arkansas and Memphis.

For the most part, folks living in the zone ignored the possibility that a major quake could occur. That is until climatologist Iben Browning predicted a fifty per cent chance of a massive quake occurring on Monday, December, 3, 1990. Although no one had successfully predicted the date a quake would occur, for some reason people living in the area believed him. Widespread concern, almost to the point of panic, took hold.

My mother at the time of the prediction lived in the quake zone in Marmaduke, Arkansas, in Northeast Arkansas. When I visited her for Thanksgiving that year, she was busy preparing for the December quake. Although I didn't believe the prediction, I did secure her gas water heater to the wall with metal straps. The securing of the tank was recommended by "quake experts."

Mama had a list of suggested things to be done to prepare for the disaster. She told me, "They said to do this or to do that." I asked her who "They" were and as always when asked that question, she didn't know. She laughed at herself for believing information from an unknown source that for the most part was told to her secondhand from ladies in her beauty shop.

My mother and her friends had collected water in gallon milk jugs. If the quake hit, they would need the water. My mother had several gallons stored underneath the dining room buffet. The nearby Walmart in Paragould was selling earthquake kits that contained survival items including dried food, candles, a Bic lighter, and a heavy-duty industrial grade flashlight. My mother had purchased a kit "just in case."

**Above: My mother and Mavis in the beauty shop**
**Below left: Mavis and her dog Tippie    Below right: New Madrid Fault**

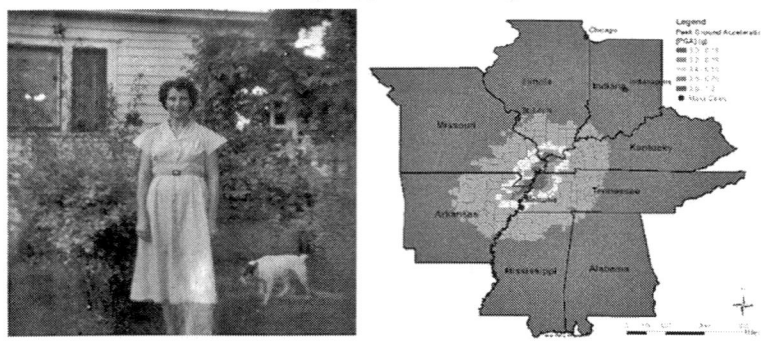

Mavis, a lady that worked for my mother, was one of the most fearful of my mother's friends about the impending doom. The night of December 3rd, she moved her car from the carport, and loaded it with supplies. Leaving her stubborn husband in the house, Mavis and her dog Tippie slept in the car on the night of great danger. She wasn't going to let her home's roof fall on top of her and the dog.

Ignoring Mavis' warning to vacate her house, my mother refused to sleep in her car that night. However, she did sleep with a pillow covering her head in case the ceiling fell in.

No earthquake occurred that night. Despite massive preparations by thousands of people in the area, most residents were saying, "I knew nothing was going to happen."

My mother said, "Well at least I got a new flashlight out of it."

**Framed:** In the early '90s I was asked to participate in a benefit art show for the Nerman Museum of Contemporary Art in Johnson County, Kansas. There were approximately 90 artists and celebrities from across the United States that were asked to participate. I was very flattered to be included in a show with some of the nation's leading artists and entertainers that included actor Martin Mull.

The theme of the show was "Frame of Mind." Each participant was given a plain wooden frame of unpainted pine, approximately two foot square with a one-foot square opening in the center. We could do with the frame anything that we felt like doing and that included totally destroying it. That's exactly what some of the artists did.

I had participated in an earlier auction for the museum and, I knew the sophisticated buying audience in the area enjoyed artworks that were cutting-edge and a little bit naughty. My finished art piece had a somewhat risqué photo in the center. I adhered cast body parts to the exterior. I was pleased when it sold for a good price.

Above: William Burroughs       Above: Frame detail

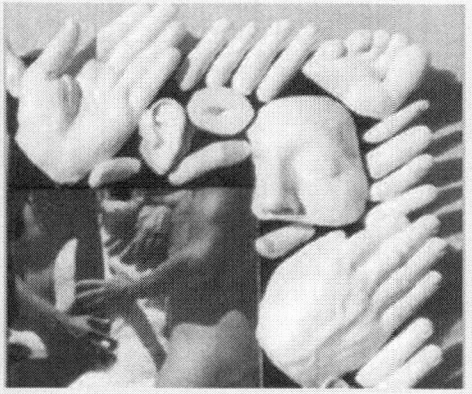

Included in that show was a piece donated by William Burroughs, who was a major postmodernist author. He is considered "one of the most culturally influential, and innovative artists of the 20th century." Burroughs is probably best known for his book, "Naked Lunch," and he is one of the founders of the Beat Generation. At the time of the show, he was living in Lawrence, Kansas, not too far from Johnson County.

I was very excited about his participation, but alas, the night of the reception, bad health kept him from attending.

Shortly after Labor Day 1951 in Mexico City, Burroughs accidentally killed his second wife, Joan Vollmer, by shooting her in the head in what was apparently a drunken attempt at playing William Tell. For the museum benefit, Burroughs had white washed his frame, placed a piece of plywood in the center, and shot a hole in the plywood with a gun. He signed it, and titled it "After Labor Day." The piece brought more than $7,000. Although somewhat morbid, I do regret not being able to buy the piece, more for the signature than for any other reason. Burroughs passed away in 1997.

Mr. Burroughs was definitely a "bad boy." There are times that being bad pays off. However, I'm not willing to take that chance

**Just Smile:** Dick and I were in Fayetteville eating lunch when one of my crowns came off. At the time I thought it was just the crown, but when I looked at it, I found the tooth was still inside the cap. One of my lateral incisors, the tooth next to the big tooth, had broken off at the gum line. I had been having what I thought were sinus problems, but as it turned out, the pain on that side of my face was due to the rotten tooth.

It was late October when my tooth broke, and two days before Halloween when hundreds of trick or treaters would be visiting my home. I also had an art reception to attend that weekend, and I was scheduled to be a poll worker at an election the following Tuesday.

Besides those obligations, I had a reporter and photographer from a national magazine, "The Crafts Report," coming to my house the following Wednesday to interview me. Not only was the reporter going to interview me, she was going to take photographs that would be included in the article.

I called my dentist who could not see me until the following Wednesday afternoon. I was mortified. My vanity would not allow me to be seen with a tooth missing. I still had the crown. I decided that I would "fix it" myself until I could see my dentist.

I went to Walmart and bought two-part epoxy. I was aware of the material's possible toxic qualities, but I was desperate. I knew that when the two substances in the epoxy were mixed together, they would harden even in a moist situation. In this case, the moist situation was my mouth.

I mixed the epoxy, pressed it into a form that fit my palate, stuck the tooth in it, and made a partial. It seemed to work fairly well, but every now and then, the partial would slip out of place. I went back to Walmart, bought a dental adhesive, and temporarily glued my homemade partial into place.

Because of the strong chemical taste I decided to only put the partial in my mouth when in public. At home, I refrained from looking in the mirror. One problem that I was having, was talking correctly. The homemade partial interfered with my tongue placement. Before meeting the public, I put the partial in my mouth a few times and practiced speaking. I felt like Demosthenes the ancient Greek Orator who practiced speaking with pebbles in his mouth. With practice, I was able to speak clearly.

All went well through each event. And the homemade partial stayed in place. The partial got me through Halloween trick or treating, the art reception, and working at the election polls. However, I was still worried about the upcoming magazine interview and the photo. It too went well.

Immediately following the magazine interview, I called a friend. While talking on the phone, my porcelain crown dislodged from the partial and fell to the kitchen floor. We both laughed. I was quite relieved that the tooth hadn't plopped out during the interview.

That afternoon, I made it to the dentist. He performed a root canal, placed a metal spike in what was left of the tooth, and attached a good looking false tooth to the spike. My dentist said, "This is a first. I've never had a client make their own partial." I thought to myself, "Yes, necessity really is the mother of invention."

Zeek Taylor, at home in his studio. Taylor is known for his stylized watercolors. One of his favorites, pictured behind him, presides over the studio.

Left, Pic that was in the mag.

Top right: Mag cover

Right: the new tooth

**Wasn't Aware that I Wasn't Aware**: I first met Gaye Adegbalola when she came to Eureka Springs to perform during the Blues Festival in 1990. She was a member of the very popular blues group "Saffire the Uppity Blues Women." Gaye and I hit it off immediately.

One time while visiting my home, Gaye noticed a picture of Dick and me that we had made in one of the photo studios downtown. In the photo, Dick and I were dressed in Confederate uniforms with a Rebel flag in the background. Being a southerner, I thought nothing of the setting. I was unaware.

*Dick, Gaye, and Zeek*

Gaye kindly confronted me about the photo. She explained that for her, an African-American women, the Confederate flag represented racism and oppression. I was heartbroken that I had offended her. I broke down and cried. I loved her so much and I could not stand the fact that I was insensitive to anything that may have hurt her. She taught me a valuable lesson about sensitivity.

Since that time I have tried to be aware, stay awake, and always consider what may offend or hurt someone. I thank Gaye for creating that awareness in me. She wrote a song, "It's Alright For A Man To Cry." She told me about the song after I had cried over hurting her.

Tears can be cleansing.

**New Bride-to-Be in Hiding**: Since 1987, I have lived across the street from the Old Stone Store on White Street in Eureka Springs, Arkansas. The building is divided into four apartments. I have seen dozens and dozens of renters come and go during that time. Some have kept to themselves, and others have been good neighbors who have become friends. The line from the "Tinker Tailor" nursery rhyme perhaps best describes the diversity of folks who have lived there: "Rich Man, Poor Man, Beggar Man, Thief, Doctor, Lawyer, Indian Chief."

Several years ago, a man who was renting a small apartment in the building called and asked if I would cut his hair, give him a manicure, and a pedicure. I said "yes" to the cut, but I told him he needed to do his own nails. He told me that he needed to look his best because he recently had become engaged to a woman whom he had met online. They had not met in person. He wanted to look good when she arrived the next week from California. I asked him if he had sent a photo of himself to her. He said, "Yes, it was a recent picture of me, and she liked my looks." I wondered if he had smiled in the photo and if she knew that he was toothless.

Soon after Jayme, the bride-to-be, arrived in Arkansas, she walked across the street to my yard sale. The groom-to-be was with her. When introduced, it was immediately evident that Jayme was a man. She was quite large, shaped like a football player, and she had hairy arms. She had on a disheveled large red wig that looked like a bad thrift store find. It was painful to hear Jayme try to elevate her voice to a higher register.

Jayme spent many afternoons that summer strolling up and down White Street. She was often accompanied by a neighbor's teenage daughter who was spending the summer in Eureka Springs. The two were kindred spirits at least when it came to dress: Daisy Duke cut-off shorts and halter tops. Their wardrobe did differ when it came to shoes. The young girl wore sandals while Jayme sensibly wore tennis shoes. I think she may have had trouble finding women's sandals in a size fifteen.

One evening an ambulance arrived at the neighbor's apartment. I went across the street while worrying that something could be seriously wrong with one of the tenants. The paramedics were at the engaged couple's apartment. The EMT workers could not maneuver the gurney into the apartment. They had to aid the afflicted out of the apartment onto the porch. They came out with Jayme and placed her on the gurney. She had on a t-shirt, cut-off short shorts, and one shoe. I noticed that she wasn't wearing her breasts, and her wig was on sideways. The next morning, I talked with the groom-to-be, and he told me that Jayme was fine. She had suffered a panic attack, and she had stayed overnight in the hospital for observation.

I didn't see her again. I thought that maybe she was staying inside to fully recover from her "bout." A few days later I read in the local paper, "James (name withheld,) aka Jayme, a female impersonator, was arrested by the FBI for computer hacking. He was taken into custody while in female attire." Jayme was extradited to California. Not too long after the arrest, I noticed that the groom-to-be's scooter was gone. I wondered if he had moved to California to be near Jayme.

When incognito, one should at the least be willing to purchase a good wig.

**Purple Muumuu and Big Lashes:** Each time Millie rang my doorbell, I knew it was her before opening the door. I could see little else but purple through the frosted panes of the stained glass in my front door. She was a very large woman who always wore a purple muumuu. She also sported a dyed black Cleopatra hairstyle with a couple of inches of white new growth showing. She wore extremely long false eyelashes that touched her eyebrows. The lashes were always crooked. Millie was an antique picker from Neosho, Missouri. In the late '80s and early '90s, she visited Eureka Springs each week to peddle her goods to the town's antique store owners.

Even though I was not an antique dealer, she stopped by my house to show me each week's "must have" finds. I think someone told her that I was an easy mark. She always said, "I saw this, thought of you, and just had to bring it to you." I later learned that was her standard spill. Even though I suspected that Millie was working me, I really liked the funny and sweet women. I sensed a good heart.

Millie drove a very old, large, olive-colored station wagon. She was accompanied by her husband Ern. He was in poor health and never got out of the car. More than once Millie would say, "I've just got to sell something today. We are out of money and I need to buy Ern an inhaler."

When she told that sad tale, I always bought something. Usually my purchase was small items, sometimes chipped, and never anything that I needed. One time I did make a big purchase, a very large file cabinet that had belonged to an artist in California. Millie and I wrestled it out of her station wagon and sat it in my driveway. There was no way that the two of us could get it into my art studio. Dick was quite surprised when he came home to find the cabinet sitting in the driveway. I still treasure the file cabinet and it has an honored place in my studio.

During one visit, Millie informed me that she wanted to sell her home in Neosho and move to Las Vegas. She invited Dick and me to see her home in case we might know someone who possibly could be interested in it. Although I didn't know anyone thinking of relocating to that town, curiosity compelled me to go look. Also, I thought it would be fun to visit Millie in her home environment.

When Dick and I arrived at her home, our jaws dropped. The large brick home was quite grand and sat on a city block. Built in the '20s or '30s, the two story house had a portes-cochère, and the home was just under seven-thousand square feet. Upon entering, we were shocked to see the rooms filled with museum quality antiques. The items included a throne chair, countless grandfather clocks, and a royal liter lift.

If Mille had one set of fine china, she had 30 sets. The bedrooms were filled with exquisite bedroom suites. Dick offered to buy one. Millie thought about the offer, and then said, "No, not for sale." I had been looking for an epergne. Millie had dozens, but none were for sale. She told us to follow her to the basement to see items that she did have that could be purchased. The available items were the run of the mill goods that she peddled when in Eureka Springs. We realized that Millie was a hoarder who couldn't bear to let go of her good stuff.

From the large basement we took an elevator to the top floor to look at the ballroom.

We got to see some of Millie's memorabilia. She had photos of herself taken years earlier when she had worked as an exotic dancer in Vegas. She was very beautiful in the pictures.

File cabinet that I purchased from Millie. It has an honored spot in my art studio.

Early Keane Painting, originally attributed to Walter Keane. Later it was revealed that the paintings were done by his wife, Margaret.

I was impressed to learn that she had been one of the models for the early Keane paintings that were sold nationwide. I remember as a child seeing the prints of the big-eyed, dark haired girl that were sold in our local Woolworths. Millie had newspaper articles documenting her role as the black haired model. During the visit she also told us the story about a time when she lived in Tulsa, went home from work, and found one of her ex-husbands in bed with a former Miss Oklahoma. We had a good laugh about that story.

Even though Millie and Ern lived in a mansion, they spent most of their waking hours in the home's kitchen with their thirteen cats. In the kitchen there were two green Naugahyde chairs that had been shredded by kitty claws, and a small television.

Even though Millie at times was desperate for money, I understood why she wouldn't sell her priceless antiques collected over a lifetime. Sometimes it's hard to let go. After the visit, I lost track of Millie. I hope she was able to sell her house and to fulfill her dream of purchasing a double wide in Vegas and to buy a warehouse for storing her collection.

You can't judge a picker by her cover, especially when the cover is a purple muumuu.

**Stage fright:** In 2012 a friend of mine was organizing a TedX event in Bentonville. She asked me to be one of the speakers. I immediately replied, "No way, I'm not a public speaker." She said, "I'm not taking "No" for an answer right now. Please think about it."

Frankly I did not know what a Ted talk was. When I mentioned that I'd been issued the invitation, my younger and more "with it" friends were in awe, and very excited that I had been asked to do a TedX talk. Encouraged by my friend's reactions, I contacted the person who asked me to participate, and I said, "Well okay, I'll do it."

When I learned that I would have to speak without notes or a teleprompter, and without a lectern, I thought, "What the hell have I done?" I also learned that the talk, approximately ten minutes in length, would take place in front of a live audience, and would be taped. The tape would then be put online and available for viewing by a worldwide audience. Agony. I rehearsed and rehearsed for hours and hours and tested my memorization skills. The day of the talk, I was more nervous than I had ever been. However, I made the talk to a very appreciative crowd and received very kind words from other speakers and audience members.

Afterwards, I felt that I had survived the ultimate test, and that I could do anything. I believe that we all have a story to tell, or a dance to perform, or a painting to share. We just have to be brave enough to do it. Do it.

**Best Friends Forever Together:** I got my first dog when I was four-years-old. One of my earliest memories is going with my parents to a kennel on Kings Highway in Paragould, Arkansas, to select a pup. I was given full reign to make the selection. I chose a small reddish terrier. I named him Jiggs, after a character in the comic strip "Bringing Up Father."

I was a middle child and the only boy in my family. My sisters had each other as "buds." In my young mind, Jiggs was my "brother" and he was my best friend. I shared my room with him, and I told him everything. The dog was my confidant and he was my comfort when I was afraid. I could always count on Jiggs.

He was with me all the time while I lived at home, and he was the hardest family member for me to leave when I went away to college. During my sophomore year at Arkansas State University, Jiggs passed away. I was talking with my mother on the phone when she gave me the news. I cried while in the phone booth. I had lost my brother.

Through the years, I've had a few dogs including Chelsea, a chocolate poodle, Heather who was an Afghan hound, and Desiree, a peek-a-poo. Desiree was with me in Memphis, during my time in Fayetteville, AR, and finally lived with me in Eureka Springs. She lived to be 18-years-old and is buried in the backyard in my pet cemetery.

About the same time that I lost her, I also lost her companion Alice, a cat, who was also 18-years-old. Within the next few months I also lost my two other cats, Joshua and Priscilla. They were both 17-years-old.

The losses were too close and almost too much for me to deal with. I said, "I can't bear to have another pet and go through this again."

I held out for a few short years before I thought, "I want another pet." When I told Dick I wanted another one, he said, "You better get one now. You are 50 years-old, and the pet may outlive you if you delay, and that wouldn't be fair to the pet." I thought "okay," and decided to get a cat because my yard wasn't really suited for another dog.

I got a Ragdoll kitten, and named him Memphis Blue. I spoiled him rotten. I bought an A-liner travel trailer so that he could go on vacation with us. I collected state magnets for him. He had eight from places that he had visited. They were on his section of the frig. The cat had traveled with us to New Orleans and, he had walked on a leash at the Florida beach. Memphis Blue was with me for more than 16 years. I still have his ashes.

Besides Memphis, in the past few years, I've had two more cats that have passed away. The other two, Dixieland Malldean, and Opie, were also cremated. I have their ashes in nice wooden boxes. I still have three cats and when they pass, I will also have them cremated.

Dick and I have lived in Eureka Springs for a long time. It is home. We want to stay here. A few years ago as a Christmas present to each other, we pooled money and bought a plot in the Eureka Springs cemetery. We plan to be cremated, and our remains will be buried there. We will also have the "cremains" of our pets buried with us. We want to stay together.

Perhaps our tombstone should read, "Merry Christmas to all and to all a good night." And that includes our fur babies.

Above left: Zeek with Jiggs
Above Center: with Chelsea
Above right: with Desiree
Lower left: Dick, Zeek, travel trailer, and Memphis Blue
Lower Center: Cemetery
Lower right: with Memphis Blue

**Happily Ever After:** Dick and I had been together 43 years when on May 9th, 2014, Circuit Judge Chris Piazza ruled the Arkansas ban on same-sex marriage invalid. The ruling came late on a Friday after courthouses in the state had closed. I was attending an art reception when I heard the news. I immediately called Dick, told him about the ruling, and said, "Do you want to get married in the morning?" He asked, "Is this a proposal?" I laughed and said, "Hell yes." He then said, "Yes, I will marry you."

The Eureka Springs' courthouse was the only one in Arkansas that would be open the next day, a Saturday. The resort town is a marriage destination. Our courthouse opens for four hours on Saturdays to accommodate tourists wanting a license. I knew that folks from all over the state would be flocking to town the next day to obtain one. I told Dick that we would get to the courthouse bright and early the next morning.

The evening before our big day, a representative from the Human Rights Campaign called and asked if one of their reporters could follow us through the licensing process and the marriage ceremony. I thought it would be nice to have the historical day documented and I said, "Yes."

I planned for us to get the license, have a nice luncheon, followed by an outdoor wedding on our patio. Prior to getting too far along with the plans, I was notified that a stay would probably be issued that could put the judge's ruling on hold. I called former mayor Beau Satori who was to conduct the ceremony, and asked him to be at the courthouse early the next morning. I told him "if" we were able to secure the license, we would be wed immediately and have the marriage recorded on the spot.

We did get to the courthouse early the next morning. There were two female couples in line ahead of us. Soon many more couples arrived and the line grew very long. The Human Rights Campaign reporter and camera person found us. We waited for the clerk to arrive. Word spread that the county clerk was "out of town," and a deputy clerk would be issuing the marriage licenses.

When the deputy clerk arrived at 9 a.m., she said she would not issue licenses to same sex couples, but she would issue them only to "normal couples." She said she did not have the proper authority. Knowing this was a possibility, I came prepared. I had printed out the judge's fourteen page ruling. I said, "Here is the ruling." She still refused. The female couples were crying. I was angry that we were having our rights denied.

When the deputy clerk opened the door, I told everyone to get in line. We filed in and lined up at the window to get our licenses. The clerk still refused. She called the police. Several policemen arrived. The clerk shut the window in our face. The police told us to leave or be arrested.

The Human Rights Campaign's camera continued to roll and the reporter continued to interview me. Dick, my friends, and I were the last ones standing our ground inside the courthouse, but eventually we too were forced to leave. Dick and a friend of mine, Cyd King, went to our home to take care of the food and drink that Cyd had brought with her from Fayetteville. It was food and drink that was to be our wedding feast.

I walked to my nearby car. Someone yelled, "Zeek, come back." Upon my return, the police informed us that the courthouse would reopen in ten minutes. Another deputy clerk who was at the courthouse to register early voters, had kindly stepped forward to issue the licenses.

I called Dick and told him to come back to the courthouse. We got back in line in the same order that we were in hours earlier. Dick and I were in line directly behind the two female couples. We were the first male couple to receive a marriage license in Arkansas, or in any southern state.

We immediately walked down a hallway to a bay window. We were joined by several of our close friends. The HRC cameras were still rolling. Our friend Beau conducted a beautiful ceremony. There were many tears. We immediately had the license recorded. We were legally married.

Dick and I are honored to have been the first male couple to be married in the South. We are forever a part of history. We were finally able to gain the rights, our civil rights, and the legal protections that marriage offers. After more than four decades together, our loving, committed relationship is recognized as "equal." We knew it all along.

Love wins in the end.

Zeek Taylor

**Love Wins**

# ABOUT THE AUTHOR

Zeek Taylor is a recipient of the Arkansas Art's Council's Governor's Arts Award for Lifetime Achievement. Best known for his stylized watercolors, the native Arkansan has won numerous awards including several "Best of Show" awards. Taylor gave a TEDx talk in Bentonville, Arkansas. He was featured on the "Tales From the South" radio show and his story, interview, and Q&A session were heard by 130 million listeners worldwide. His StoryCorps interview on NPR's Morning Edition show was heard by 50 million listeners nationwide. The StoryCorps interview, conducted with Dick Titus, is on file in the Library of Congress. Taylor lives and works in Eureka Springs, Arkansas.
His work may be viewed at www.zeektaylor.com

Made in the USA
Middletown, DE
24 September 2022